THE TROUBLE WITH WAGNER

THE TROUBLE WITH WAGNER

MICHAEL P. STEINBERG

THE UNIVERSITY OF CHICAGO PRESS
Chicago and London

The University of Chicago Press, Chicago 60637
The University of Chicago Press, Ltd., London
© 2018 by The University of Chicago
All rights reserved. No part of this book may be used or reproduced in any manner whatsoever without written permission, except in the case of brief quotations in critical articles and reviews. For more information, contact the University of Chicago Press, 1427 E. 60th St., Chicago, IL 60637.
Published 2018
Printed in the United States of America

27 26 25 24 23 22 21   2 3 4 5

ISBN-13: 978-0-226-59419-4 (cloth)
ISBN-13: 978-0-226-59422-4 (e-book)
DOI: https://doi.org/10.7208/chicago/9780226594224.001.0001

Library of Congress Cataloging-in-Publication Data
Names: Steinberg, Michael P., author.
Title: The trouble with Wagner / Michael P. Steinberg.
Description: Chicago ; London : The University of Chicago Press, 2018. | Includes bibliographical references and index.
Identifiers: LCCN 2018022863 | ISBN 9780226594194 (cloth : alk. paper) | ISBN 9780226594224 (e-book)
Subjects: LCSH: Wagner, Richard, 1813–1883. Ring des Nibelungen. | Wagner, Richard, 1813–1883—Criticism and interpretation.
Classification: LCC ML410.W15 S74 2018 | DDC 782.1092—dc23
LC record available at https://lccn.loc.gov/2018022863

♾ This paper meets the requirements of ANSI/NISO Z39.48-1992 (Permanence of Paper).

For my family

CONTENTS

Preface ix

INTRODUCTION
Wagnerian Songlines
1

ONE
History and the Stage
35

TWO
Siegmund's Death
60

THREE
Bad Education
82

FOUR
Les passions humaines
101

AFTERWORD
On Purity, Danger, and the Postsecular Moment
126

Acknowledgments 139

Notes 143

Index 149

PREFACE

This book weaves together two distinct strands of experience, thinking, and writing. The first involves years of listening to the works under discussion here—Wagner's *Der Ring des Nibelungen*, mostly, but also the three late operas—*Tristan und Isolde*, *Die Meistersinger von Nürnberg*, and *Parsifal*, integrating them along the way into an academic and occasional public curriculum of teaching, lecturing, and writing. Works of art and imagination of this kind of breadth and depth function as agents and drivers of cultural and political history at least as much as they do as autonomous formal entities, on the one hand, or as mirrors or symptoms of their times, on the other. The responsibility to form and the commitment to context together build the practice of what has come to be known as the cultural history of music. The second strand making its way through the book comes out of the more hands-on experience of my role as a dramaturg, or conceptual advisor, on the staging of the *Ring* coproduced by the Teatro alla Scala Milano and the Berlin State Opera between 2010 and 2013.

This double story now seeks to blend two kinds of writing. First, the analysis and interpretation of the texts (words and music) and some of their significant contexts—in other words the kind of interdisciplinary reading that would be appropriate to a scholarly project or classroom and also similar to the perspective and content through which I engaged the production team during the periods of conceptual preparation and into some of the rehearsal periods. Second, a kind of memoir of the production itself: what I take it to have been arguing, how it developed, how it worked and, sometimes, how it didn't. Since its completion in 2013, Guy Cassiers's production has been revived once in its entirety—in Berlin in 2016. To my knowledge it will not be revived again. However, its availability on DVD and on YouTube extends its life. Usually, therefore, but not always, I refer to the production in the past tense.

The chapters are also constructed somewhat diversely. The introduction pursues key aesthetic, historical, and theoretical components of the *Ring* and of the claims and ideologies of Wagnerian music drama. It can be read sequentially and/or referentially, in the latter way as its various sections relate to the discussions of the later chapters. The four central chapters focus on the works, or evenings, of the tetralogy of the *Ring*: *Das Rheingold* (The Gold of the Rhine), *Die Walküre* (The Valkyrie), *Siegfried*, and *Götterdämmerung* (Twilight of the Gods). The afterword offers briefer, more episodic treatments of the three late music dramas (*Tristan*, *Meistersinger*, and *Parsifal*) in the context of some thoughts about the evolution and some current aspects of the question of the "post-secular" and the return of the sacred to modern culture and society.

I do assume the reader's basic familiarity with the plots of the operas, summaries of which are easily available. I do not assume any deep knowledge of how music drama works, of which an account is the main responsibility of the introduction.

Kernels of chapters 1–4 first appeared as short essays in the program books of the La Scala and Berlin productions of the four *Ring* operas (in the agreement that expanded versions would be published subsequently). An earlier version of a portion of chapter 2 as well as passages from chapters 3 and 4 appeared in the chapter "The Family Romances of Music Drama" in my book *Listening to Reason: Culture and Subjectivity in Nineteenth-Century Music* (Princeton University Press, 2004). A preliminary version of a portion of the afterword appeared in the essay "Music Drama and the End of History," *New German Critique*, no. 69 (Fall 1996).

INTRODUCTION

Wagnerian Songlines

In late 2019 the Jewish Museum Berlin will unveil an entirely new permanent exhibition covering the history of Jewish life in Germany, from the Middle Ages to the present day. In planning the complex narrative of the modern period—from the age of emancipation and enlightenment in the mid to late eighteenth century, through reunification in 1870 and the victory of nationalism over liberalism, to the political victory of National Socialism in 1933 and the work of reconstruction after 1945—the curatorial team intends to give unique focus to a single individual: Richard Wagner.

Two claims are implicit here. First, "the case of Wagner" emerges as fundamental to the lives of German Jews: to their mediation with the social majority, to their aesthetic and political taste and intimacy and their identification with German traditions and forms. Second, "Wagner and the Jews" becomes paradigmatic for the German struggle between mythical and myth-based unity on the one side, and the realities of cultural diversity on the other. In the demographic dimension of this structure, the Jews constitute roughly 3 percent of the population. The Christian population remains evenly divided between Catholics and Protestants, a division that had to be suppressed if national unity was to take hold both politically and emotionally. The perfect political storm of anti-Semitism can thus be understood as a displacement of suppressed intra-Christian difference. Richard Wagner resides, then and now, at the center of that storm. More than that, he largely defines it. Wagner's career etches the claim to cultural unity and its violence, while at the same time disclosing lines of critique and self-critique with the potential at least to reintroduce a strand of humanity into that dubious agenda.

Wagner's later music dramas are to my ear unequalled for the beauty and knowledge with which they engage the world. The power of their literary and musical sources notwithstanding, they amount to fully original phenomena that evolve together with their governing aesthetic category of music drama. *Der Ring des Nibelungen*, the main focus here, occupied Wagner from the initial sketches of 1848 up to the premiere of the full tetralogy in 1876, inaugurating the composer's self-celebratory Bayreuth Festival. For its admirers and detractors alike, the *Ring* holds a unique place in Wagner's work and in the history of music and drama for its claim to tell the story of the world itself. At the same time, these same works remain fundamentally vulnerable to Friedrich Nietzsche's disavowal of them on the claim that "music should not become an art of lying." If music can lie, Nietzsche's charge presumes, then music can also tell the truth. My point: Wagner in his music and music drama both tells the truth and lies. He does so simultaneously. This is the Wagnerian reality. The paradox begins and lodges inside the music drama: "*IN* IT," to invoke Anna Russell's immortal syllables. The virtually universal avoidance of this problem among Wagner's devotees, detractors, and interpreters, both scholarly and popular—the drive somehow to separate the good Wagner from the bad, whether by distancing the man from the work, the prose writings from the creative work, by hailing the good exception of *Tristan und Isolde* or the bad exception of *Parsifal*—does not and cannot hold.

1. The Problem

In March 1983, the year of the centennial of Richard Wagner's death, I had the pleasure of teaching a mini-seminar (a "work group," in the local parlance) on Richard Wagner's *Ring des Nibelungen* for Princeton University's European Cultural Studies program. Our focus was *Die Walküre* and the god Wotan's struggle between the privileges of traditional sovereignty and the burdens of modern social contracts. The discussions were lively and rigorous, and I took away from them the lesson of how well Wagner teaches its way into key issues of the modern world: its politics, its aesthetics, its dense landscapes of progress and decay, freedom and injustice, beauty and violence, human wisdom and human degradation. The problem was that Wagner—the man, the mind, the music, the phenomenon—appeared on all sides of these sets of dialectics. Wagner the perpetrator always shadows Wagner the visionary.

At the conclusion of our sessions, the students and I attended a peculiarly narcoleptic traversal of *Die Walküre* at the Metropolitan Opera, apparently the company's best effort in that centennial year. No element of the revival had anything to say about the work—a fatal flaw. For us that sea-son, the Wagner classroom proved far more exciting than the Wagner stage or pit. No matter; I retained then, as I still do now, the abiding example of the potential of Wagner in performance.

In the summer of 1976 and as a college student myself, I had managed to snag a jettisoned ticket to the premiere run of Patrice Chéreau's *Götterdämmerung* at the centennial Bayreuth Festival. (The ticket was one among about a dozen ejected from a cortege of Mercedes-Benz sedans by a chain of elegant dowagers taking part in an organized action against the alleged sacrileges of Chéreau's production and Pierre Boulez's conducting—about which more later.) I think that performance changed my life. In any case, it still energizes me today. It exemplified the combination of *Werktreue* (loyalty to the work) with the radical rediscovery of the same work as a fresh font of knowledge. To put the *Ring* on a stage, I learned then, you need to have something to say—about the work itself, about its world and ours, and about the gaps between them.

Thirty years later, during the Wagner bicentennial year of 2013, I again taught a seminar to an equally inspiring group of students. Not for the first time, I called the course "The Case of Wagner." The course title is a clear reference to Nietzsche's "Turinese Letter of 1888," the most devastating of his later-career indictments of the man he had previously adulated. Nietzsche's short text is as negative as his early *Birth of Tragedy from the Spirit of Music* (1871) is positive. They are equally incisive and analytical, and we read both in the class. This time, however, a typographical error found its way into the course catalog, so that the class was mistakenly announced as "The Case *for* Wagner." The accident proved a happy one, as it allowed me to introduce the semester according to the need to steer between "the case of," with its call to diagnosis, analysis, and judgment (whether legal, psychological, or neither), and "the case for" and its suggestion of advocacy. After thirty years of teaching and more than forty since Bayreuth 1976, I still feel like a beginner in the company of this material. The chance to converse with inspired students in or close to their first exposure is therefore always what I enjoy most. Thirty years of listening, thinking, writing, and teaching make for one of the two archives at the base of this short book.

The second and equally important source is more recent and involves my work on the Berlin-Milan coproduction of the *Ring* between 2009 and 2013. The production was conducted by Daniel Barenboim and staged by Guy Cassiers and his team of production artists associated with the Toneelhius Theater of Antwerp. *Das Rheingold* and *Die Walküre* premiered in Milan in May and December 2010 and moved on to Berlin; *Siegfried* and *Götterdämmerung* opened in Berlin in 2012 and 2013. Berlin offered three full cycles of the tetralogy in March–April 2013; Milan offered two in June. My initial work took place in a bare conference room in Antwerp, where, over four long weekends spread out over the same number of years, a group of us discussed the mammoth work, developed some of the production's concepts, and planned their visual as well as human materializations for the stage. The conversations there resembled those of a lively classroom; the result, however, beyond the proverbial set of term papers, was a major, indeed possibly historic production.

The learning curve for me was steep, and it continued to climb when we reached rehearsals and the adaptation of ideas to the abilities, wills, and idiosyncrasies of the performers as well as to the innumerable contingencies of life in an opera house. For example, from my observations of and interactions with the singers and their radically individualized confrontations with Wagner's text, I developed a fresh fascination with Wagner's words. I had long ago drunk the potion of the music while sustaining the standard scholarly condescension to Wagner's texts and poetics. My respect for the singers' work and challenges of memorization and articulation occasioned at least a partial destabilization of the operatic (though decidedly not Wagnerian) hierarchy of *prima la musica, poi le parole*.

The rehearsals were events, textual and contextual. First, the spiraling challenges of mounting this gigantic four-part work. Secondly, the encounter of the work and the production concept with the unparalleled rigor and knowledge of Daniel Barenboim, whose every decision and instruction is a lesson in the arguments and capacities of musical forms. The orchestra of the Teatro alla Scala is a first-rate symphonic ensemble with a distinguished concertizing history and profile, as is of course the Staatskapelle Berlin, which also functions as the orchestra of the Berlin State Opera. For the La Scala musicians, the *Ring* is another country's music, and many of the players were confronting it for the first time. The same is true for the La Scala audiences. In Italy, Wagner is someone else's problem. For the Berliners, Wagner is decidedly homegrown—but therein lies a deeper problem. The unique embeddedness of the Wagner legacy in modern German history and in the history of the Third Reich and its aftermath informs and indeed even obsesses every German return to this material. The stage and musical histories of these works after 1945 are intensely self-conscious and problematic, producing a unique history of production values (as I'll discuss in the first chapter). Cassiers and his team thus took on the vexing but intensely interesting challenge of building a cycle for both Milan and

Berlin, Italy and Germany, one that had to be both lyrical and beautiful as well as historically truthful if it was to satisfy the tastes and anxieties of these two different houses and two different cultures. Acted out on a practical basis in the evolution of the production, the politico-operatic case of Germany versus Italy forms a key subtext to the *Ring* itself as well as to the specific history of the Milan-Berlin production.

Barenboim's orchestra rehearsals in Berlin and the musical education they offer are known draws of practitioners and scholars. His *Ring* OPs (*Orchesterproben*, or orchestra rehearsals) and BOs (*Bühne-Orchester*, or stage orchestra [rehearsals]) were attended by three generations of conductors and other musical figures: patriarchs, their students, and their students' students. In this group, Israelis were overrepresented, as they are in Berlin generally. Unreliable estimates notwithstanding, Berlin is today the domicile of some eleven thousand Israelis, among them apparently up to three thousand musicians. Aware of Wagner's indispensability to the concert repertoire, Israeli classical musicians attended these rehearsals because Barenboim and Berlin's Wagner is so deeply considered, reflective, and authoritative, and because Wagner is not played in Israel—the object, as is well-known, of a cultural taboo (see chapter 5).

In a thoughtful essay titled "Wagner, Israel, and the Palestinians," Barenboim offers some insights into some of the structural and technical aspects of Wagner's musical texture, the relation between calculation and effect, and the relation between musical style and ideological content. I will address the latter issues in chapter 5, and with some disagreement at that. Here it's worth foregrounding two key musical insights that offer a clue to the way Barenboim instructs the orchestra. These are, first, the mathematical relation of economy of means to power of effect and, secondly, the distinction between the complex and the complicated. On the first issue, Barenboim notes that Wagner opens the first act of *Die Walküre* with a storm depicted in music, but that unlike his hero Beethoven, who depicted a storm in his *Pastoral* Symphony by marshaling the full power and variety of his orchestra, Wagner paints his storm only with string instruments. This economy of sound allows the emphasis of the mathematical arc of crescendo-to-climax through the intensification of musical phrases or ideas—first in two bars, next in a two-bar repetition followed by an instruction of *subito piano*, and then in a four-bar crescendo followed by a climax. "It is therefore a mathematical equation," Barenboim writes, "that gives rise to sensuality and fervor."

Barenboim's distinction between the complex and the complicated rests on a grammatical insight. "Wagner's music is often complex," he writes, "sometimes simple, but never complicated." Barenboim associates complexity with multidimensionality, in other words a state of reality that can be questioned phenomenologically, rather than a state deliberately produced. To make something complex for its own sake is to complicate it. Something complicated has been made so—the word "complicated" is, strictly speaking, a verb participle rather than an adjective.[1]

Indispensability is the first problem with Wagner. Matters of taste aside, the so-called classical tradition in music, as its makes its way through the nineteenth century (ever its most popular century for audiences), cannot be understood historically, empirically, or formally without Wagner. The removal of Wagner from the repertoire is thus a cognitive violation, analogous to a coy pedagogical trick that I recall from a middle-school grammar textbook that coddled the presumed Luddism of its young student victims by suggesting the experimental removal of one or more of the eight parts of speech and then showing that language proved nonviable without all eight. Taste and interest do, however, inform the assertion, by no means made by everyone, that Wagner is indispensable to modern understandings of the human condition.

The work that occupied Richard Wagner for more than a quarter of a century, spurring his own self-sacralization and self-institutionalization (in the form of the Bayreuth Festival, which opened in 1876 with the full cycle that included the world premieres of *Siegfried* and *Götterdämmerung*), amounts to the measure of modernist achievement both in its own right and in relation to the innumerable efforts in multiple genres that necessarily measure themselves—intentionally or functionally—in relation to it. When Charles Baudelaire coined the term "modernity" in 1859 as "the fleeting, the transitory, and the contingent," and thus "one side of art, the other of which is the absolute and the immovable," he was writing about the draftsman Constantin Guys, who exemplified the first side of the equation, but he was likely thinking also about his hero Wagner, who exemplified both sides. Within several months he wrote the music criticism that finally established Wagner's status as the preeminent modernist in Paris. When Wagner brought the new version of *Tannhäuser* to Paris—now with the Venusberg scene presented as a potently narcotic riff on the generic ballet episode that the city's operatic convention required—along with several concerts, including the prelude to act 1 of *Lohengrin*, which particularly entranced Baudelaire, he had already completed the score of *Tristan und Isolde*, the masterpiece that, along with *Die Meistersinger von Nürnberg*, resulted from the long hiatus away from the *Ring*. When Wagner returned to the composition of the *Ring* (picking up with act 3 of *Siegfried*), he infused its musical vocabulary with the prime dividend of *Tristan*, namely music's claim to have become the language of the unconscious. For post-Wagnerian modernists in many genres, from music to literature, painting, stagecraft, and so on, modernism's radicality articulated the will to get underneath language and consciousness, to recapture the lost human foundations of myth. In the Wagnerian inventory, this program is established by the *Ring* plus *Tristan*.

From 1839 to 1846 Wagner sought the support of Giacomo Meyerbeer (born Jakob Beer in Berlin), the reigning grand opera composer in Paris. Meyerbeer helped to finance and arrange performances of *Rienzi* and *Tannhäuser* in Dresden but turned down a loan request in 1846, a refusal that raised Wagner's hackles. His resentment about Meyerbeer's influence appears to have exacerbated long-held anxieties about true and false fathers, fanning the therapeutic strategy of delegitimating rejecting fathers as inauthentic to begin with. Such delegitimation of a "false" father figure appears as a negative version of the family romance (the invention of a false lineage to suggest noble descent). In the 1840s and '50s, anti-Judaism, which on the bases of new racialist and linguistic cosmologies was being potently retooled as the pseudo-scientific discourse of anti-Semitism, proved an accurate weapon for such negative romances, both on the individual, biographical and autobiographical level and on the macro, cultural level. It was easy enough to reclaim Judaism in the most global terms as the false parent of Christianity. For Wagner, the case of Meyerbeer, doubled by that of Felix Mendelssohn, built the paradigm that he theorized in the 1850 essay *Das Judentum in der Musik* (*Judaism in Music*). The cultural inauthenticity of the Jews, Wagner argued (at first under the flashy pseudonym "K. Freigedank" but under his own name in the second edition), foreclosed on their potential as creators and artists, though it allowed them to excel as interpreters of the art of others. Chronologically, then, *Judaism in Music* emerges simultaneously with the text of the *Ring*. A long-lived scholarly stalemate has failed to resolve the question of the presence and relevance of Wagner's anti-Judaism to his own creative work and to the *Ring* in particular. We can, indeed must, begin by breaking through this impasse, by avoiding the quicksand of easily claimed and dubiously sustained middle grounds.

2. Dividing by Zero

In their book *Finding an Ending*, Philip Kitcher and Richard Schacht stake out that middle ground deliberately:

> Negative judgments about Wagner and the *Ring* are, as we have noted, quite common. Some are obviously grounded in reactions to the man (rather than being based directly on a response to his work). Scholars as well as many others have written at length about Wagner's anti-Semitism and chauvinistic German nationalism—and there is no doubt that his views about Jews were thoroughly vile. Whether the anti-Semitism pervades his music dramas in general and the *Ring* in particular, however, is a much more difficult question. Although some Wagnerian characters are often taken to present Jews as conniving, base, contemptible, or detestable—the favorite candidates being Beckmesser in *Meistersinger* and Mime in the *Ring*—our view is that the identification of these characters as portraying Jews already presupposes prejudicial stereotypes.[2]

But the point is precisely that such stereotypes *were* in place. They were cultural facts gaining ground during the period of the *Ring*'s gestation and thus increasingly attachable both by Wagner and his audiences to the modes of detestability of Mime, Beckmesser, and other characters. It is not a question of certain traits being or being claimed to be essentially, typologically, or philosophically Jewish, but rather the material, historical existence of what Shulamit Volkov authoritatively called "anti-Semitism as a cultural code." This is a matter of historical reality, not the function of an abstract or ideal construction.[3]

At the same time, there is another side to the issue, conceivably a more important one. If the conniving dwarf Mime (who raises the young Siegfried with the intention of killing him after the boy has secured the ring and golden hoard for his foster parent) and the creatively impotent critic and pedant Sixtus Beckmesser adhere to the tenets and stereotypes of anti-Semitism as a cultural code, as do Meyerbeer and Mendelssohn when framed by Wagner's portrayals, the other elements of the same code inform, more subtly and more unexpectedly, characters with fundamentally different aesthetic and moral profiles. Siegmund, the heroic erotic outsider, has a place in that code, as will be developed in chapter 2. So does Kundry, as I will show in chapter 5). The unstated Jewish inflections of the character Siegmund inspired in Wagner's audiences both instances of indulgent anti-Semitism (Thomas Mann's story "Blood of the Volsungs") as well as admiration and role modeling. No male given name proved more popular among fin-de-siècle central European Jews than Siegmund. Attribution of this practice to the desire for assimilation and to anxiety may tell part of this story, but only part. Equally important was the identification with the character Siegmund. The investment of heroic or redemptive traits as elements within Jewish characterological inflections (unstated as these may have remained) points to a substantial complication and partial deconstruction of the anti-Judaism that remains unquestionably present in Wagner's creative as well as his theoretical work. As is the case also with the reddest thread of German anti-Semitism in general, it is the identification with the Jews as in fundamental ways indistinguishable from other Germans that stokes the flames of cultural anxiety, resentment, and hatred. From *Judaism in Music* all the way to the 1947 film *Gentlemen's Agreement*, anti-Semites are most anxious when they cannot distinguish Jews from non-Jews, when Jews look and sound like Siegmund and Gregory Peck rather than like the dwarf Mime.

Wagner's anti-Judaism remains present, palpable, and perverse, and without clear boundaries. The trouble with Wagner, then, is that the works are both indispensable and perverse. The problem is also that this tension cannot be resolved. The polarity cannot be reconciled. Any effort or claim to such resolution or reconciliation strays quickly into illogic and disingenuousness and must not be undertaken if the works and their contexts are to be considered with respect to and for reality. It is a nonviable move, like dividing by zero, like — to borrow an analogy from the history of psychoanalysis — the decision that the pioneering child analyst and theorist of "playing and reality" D. W. Winnicott prohibits from being made, indeed the question that cannot be asked: whether the transitional object (the bridge or mediator between the toddler and the world in the form of a teddy bear or other object) comes from the outside world or the inner world of the child.[4]

It does not escape me that, with the assertion that the question "Can we" or "How can we reconcile Wagner's genius with his perversity, in the form of anti-Semitism" amounts to an unaskable question in Winnicott's sense, I am invoking something close to the central plot problem of *Lohengrin*: the grounding of a contract in the prohibition of a question. Because it is never my intention to underestimate Wagner's powers of insight, I think it is possible that he understood the alchemy of genius and perversity in a similar way. That he himself didn't know what to do with his anti-Semitism and perversity in relation to his genius. In any case, a sharp distinction persists between two propositions: between the question that *cannot* be asked and the one that *may not* be asked. "Nie sollst Du mich befragen," Lohengrin warns Elsa—which is, strictly speaking, neither a "can" (*kannst*) nor a "may" (*darfst*), but rather a "should" or a "must." Never must you ask me, he instructs his potential insta-bride, where I come from, what my origins are, and how they relate to my current actions, including rescuing you, marrying you, and contributing to your society. Stating his condition publicly, Lohengrin is telling both Elsa and her fellow Brabantians that his induction into their society as hero and husband—into the public and private spheres alike—must be disaggregated from the question of his origins. The question that must not be asked is the Jewish question. Here Lohengrin sidesteps the political and moral responsibility for the prohibition and its legitimacy: the difference between the suppression of a legitimate question and the recognition, including its implicit invitation of consensus, that the question can only be a mutual trap if it invokes an epistemic impossibility.

Now, in line with Anton Chekhov's maxim that if a gun appears onstage in the first act, it has to go off by the last act, we the audience can predict that Elsa will disobey Lohengrin's command in some eventual moment of crisis. Any parent knows that to mark something as forbidden is to make it irresistible. As we track Elsa's progress through the opera—and as we think about it afterward—we may still reflect on whether the rebellious question (coaxed as the question may have been by the evil Ortrud) with which she confronts her new husband is a confrontation of power or of truth. If she is refusing his prohibition of a legitimate and necessary question, she is confronting power; if he is identifying an epistemically unaskable question, she is in turn toppling a truth, a reality principle, whether driven by childishness or obsessiveness. If she is subverting a reality principle rather than someone's bad politics, she is entering a psychotic realm. I'm not sure about Lohengrin's politics here—nor about Elsa's—but I am confident that Winnicott's model identifies a cognitive trap on whose avoidance depends the ability to function in the world.

Thus the demand for impossible knowledge can take multiple forms, including the psychotic as well as the political. Acting from the wish to know death from within life is an example of the psychotic. The desire to know the death-in-life of the unconscious is in fact Tristan's predicament, as he himself confesses to King Marke:

> O König, das
> kann ich dir nicht sagen;
> und was du frägst,
> das kannst du nie erfahren....
> Dem Land, das Tristan meint,
> der Sonne Licht nicht scheint:
> es ist das dunkel
> nächt'ge Land,
> daraus die Mutter
> mich entsandt....
>
> O King, this I cannot tell you;
> And what you ask you can never experience.
> On the land that Tristan means
> No sunlight ever shines;
> It is the dark, nocturnal land
> Out from which my mother sent me....

This terrain, discovered through eros, which Tristan will now strive to understand in an act of prolonged suicide, may in fact be envisioned by Lohengrin's prohibition. Nietzsche may have got the latter wrong when he referred to it as "a solemn excommunication of inquiry" and thus a representation of "the Christian concept, 'you ought to and must *believe*.'"[5] Could Lohengrin have been advising his audience—Elsa and the Brabantians—to avoid the dark land of impossible knowledge rather than insisting on their ignorance and obedience? Could he have been saying, "In asking about origins, you are asking for false knowledge, indeed for a false reconciliation between origins and purpose; you are demanding a false reconciliation, a false identity (to use the language of Theodor Adorno, *contra* Hegel) that will compromise both truth and society." Here, irreconcilability becomes a reality principle as well as a political necessity.

Nietzsche's rejection of the excommunication of inquiry reaffirms the Enlightenment charge of Kant's motto, *sapere aude*: dare to know. The principle leaves untouched, however, the problem of cognitive possibility. Thinking into death is one such impossibility; it drives Tristan mad. In 1945 Hermann Broch attached a post-Joycean modernism to this same experiment in his novel *The Death of Virgil*, which traces the poet's last hours under the text's self-imposed, and doomed, challenge of following him into death. Not stopping at this boundary is an act of psychosis and, ultimately, death, as in the case of Tristan. It is thus inherently dangerous at a purely cognitive level, distinct from a political one. The action may be forbidden, but only because it is impossible.

In the history of mathematics, and again in the more contemporary discourse of computer science, this play between the cognitively impossible and the (politically) forbidden is evident in the problem of division by zero. Division by zero is an impossible operation. The ninth-century Jain mathematician Mahavira addresses it, as does George Berkeley in his 1734 treatise *The Analyst*. These sources generate the standard description of division by zero as an *undefined* operation, that is, one that doesn't exist. (If division is the opposite of multiplication, then it follows that a number divisible by zero must be arrived at by multiplying the result by zero. Since multiplying any number by zero always produces zero, the operation is impossible.) Recent discussions of this issue among computer scientists have shifted from a language of indefinability to a rhetoric of forbiddenness, danger, and crash, even describing as apocalyptic the potential outcome of a process that includes a division by zero. And that, finally, is precisely the finale of the first story I ever heard attached to the problem, told to an algebra class by a favorite high school teacher. Dividing by zero is not only impossible but dangerous, he warned, and the proof lies in an infamous American bridge disaster: the November 1940 collapse of the new bridge at Tacoma Narrows, Washington—the result, he claimed, of an isolated division by zero lodged somewhere within an engineer's calculation. The event was filmed by a passer-by and is easily found on YouTube.

3. Nietzsche Undone

Friedrich Nietzsche remains Richard Wagner's most fundamental and most devastating critic. At the same time his critique counts consistently as a philosophical limit experience and therefore also as a critique of philosophy and a self-critique. The young Nietzsche found inspiration and truth in Wagner, conceiving and dedicating to him his early work *The Birth of Tragedy from the Spirit of Music* (1872). The essay "Richard Wagner in Bayreuth" (1876) shows an emergent ambivalence, the result of Nietzsche's presence at a cornerstone-laying ceremony at Bayreuth and his growing suspicion of the composer's self-monumentalization. *Parsifal* (whose piano score he admired but which he never heard in performance beyond an orchestral traversal of its prelude in Monte Carlo) and Nietzsche's diagnosis not only of its recumbent Christianity but its fraudulent Christianity caused the final break, the diatribes of both *The Case of Wagner* and *Beyond Good and Evil*, and also the removal of the predicate "from the Spirit of Music" from the second and subsequent editions of *The Birth of Tragedy*. Beyond Bayreuth and *Parsifal*, nationalism and anti-Semitism hardened Nietzsche's scorn, for however we evaluate his elusive politics, his anti-nationalism and anti-anti-Semitism remained steadfast.

Yet even Nietzsche may have protested too much. Already *The Birth of Tragedy* reveals how his construction and diagnosis of the cultural options for Germany—or indeed for modernity more generally—would not allow a full escape from his Wagnerism. For the young classicist Nietzsche in 1871, Wagner's aesthetic of music drama, riding as it unquestionably did the wave of classical scholarship that had restored the form and argument of Aeschylean tragedy, grafted the civic and cultural function of tragedy onto a new and contemporary scene. Granted, the polis had morphed from the city to the nation, but this was not a problem for Nietzsche in 1871. For modern Germany as for ancient Athens, tragedy provided the founding myths that could define, bind, and motivate the polis. In both cases, tragedy's forms involved story and music. In both cases, form and its rules jockeyed with visceral identification and emotion—the Apollonian with the Dionysian, in Nietzsche's terms. And in both cases, the union of the Apollonian and the Dionysian was threatened (in the Greek case, undone) by the challenge of the Socratic, in other words by the negativity of philosophical inquiry. Nietzsche's self-identification (as a philosopher at least) reaches an ironic impasse here. *The Birth of Tragedy* and its aftermath, as Nietzsche clearly sees, cannot get past the question that is ultimately more basic than the question of Wagner: the question of myth and the mythical foundation of culture most generally. To put the problem another way: Nietzsche can argue that Wagner is the false prophet of the new mythology, but he cannot on his own terms argue that culture can function without its myths altogether. He therefore cannot allow himself to find ways in which Wagner may be striving for just that kind of more open exploration of cultural forms and political principles.

4. Ambivalence and Music Drama

The Wagnerian oeuvre is to a great extent built on tensions and dualities, predicaments that inform some significant word choices in Wagner's highly idiosyncratic language. Ambivalence (in German the more literal *Zwiespalt*, or the "split into two" [*zwei/zwie* as well as *zwischen* (between)] is a prominent predicament as well as word choice in the *Ring*. "Ich wusste den Zwiespalt, der dich zwang" (I recognized the ambivalence that forced your hand), Brünnhilde says to Wotan in act 3, scene 3 of *Die Walküre*, referring to his decision to have his son Siegmund felled in the duel with Hunding, against his own desires and plans. (I would actually prefer to translate *Zwiespalt* as some blunt neologism such as "mind-split" rather than as the gentle "ambivalence.") In his culminating exchange with Erda in act 3, scene 1 of *Siegfried*, Wotan exclaims:

> Was in des Zwiespalts wildem Schmerze
> verzweifelnd einst ich beschloss,
> froh und freudig
> führe frei ich nun aus.
>
> What once I decided in the despair of
> The wild pain of ambivalence [wild, mind-splitting pain],
> I now bring to reality
> with pleasure and joy.

The problem of the twin (*Zwilling*, which shares its root with *Zwiespalt*) is more prominent still, creating a pivot of the drama in the incestuous bond between the twins Siegmund and Sieglinde. Largest of all predicaments of ambivalence is the basic category of the entire enterprise: that of music drama itself. As the union of music and text, music drama as a category and aesthetic enterprise represents a union of siblings, and since Wagner's words carry sonic and musical messages, it is not far-fetched to speculate that this union is in fact an incestuous one. The number two (*zwei*) is at the root of the twin, and at the root of the moral and tragic ambivalence, or split (*Zwiespalt*), that Wotan will cite in the context of the Siegmund contradiction—the plan to recast society through an antisocial taboo, namely incest. Together, *Zwilling* and *Zwiespalt* function as plot elements and as formal allegories: of music and text as inseparable but possibly incestuous twins.[6]

Music drama claims to occupy the position of anti-opera. As Carl Dahlhaus reminds us, Wagner himself resisted the moniker "music drama," suspicious of its connotation of a drama for music. Yet in his treatise *Opera and Drama* (1851), he asserted that drama is the purpose and end in a relation where music is the means or medium. The claim has led to much misunderstanding, as Dahlhaus points out, most especially to the assumption that the drama must reside in the text. The relationship between music and text is especially complex in the case of the *Ring* because the text came first, written in reverse, so to speak, from the story of Siegfried's death (*Siegfrieds Tod*, as *Götterdämmerung* was originally titled) backward through the expository tales that eventually took form as *Das Rheingold*, *Die Walküre*, and *Siegfried*. In 1854, early in this history of the tetralogy's musical composition, Wagner read Arthur Schopenhauer's *The World as Will and Representation*, which supplied him with the argument for music as the unmediated language of the will. The mature texture of music drama thus argues, through form, through the actual works, that the musical discourse is primary and drives the drama, and indeed that the text is itself musicalized so that the actual sounds of the words, in particular the opening consonants, carry sonic and ideological meaning. Wagner expressed this mature, primary status of music in his 1870 centennial essay "Beethoven," asserting that, rather than *representing* an idea of the world, music *is* an idea of the world. This progression leads Dahlhaus to the Hegelian formulation that "drama is the 'formative motive' that the music needs for self-realization."[7] We might therefore list the three principles of mature music drama as follows:

1. The prime category is drama.
2. The drama is primarily musical, including the musicalization of words.
3. The musical texture is an extension of the Beethovenian symphony.

Music drama's enemy is opera. "Opera" is for Wagner both Italian and nonsensical, condemned to musical impotence by the triviality of its attached dramatic material. (Note that his condemnation carried distinctions. The villain who trashed Italian opera was, for him, Donizetti, while its redeemer was, or might have been, Bellini. There would have been no *Götterdämmerung*, as we shall see, without *Norma*. Bellini abided as the provider of the melodic ideal, the truly ineffable goal of music for Wagner, notwithstanding the enduring emphasis of German musical aesthetics on harmony.)[8] Wagner understood the error of Italian opera as the production of (trivial) music out of (trivial) drama; the triumph of his new aesthetic was to generate (great) music from (great) drama. Yet where is the boundary between text and music as the dual generators of drama? Here is the font of aesthetic ambivalence. For Wagner, the music carries authority, and the texts form a dimension of the *musical* body of the works. Though the *Ring*'s tetralogical structure would not have emerged without Johann Gustav Droysen's philological discovery of the same principle in Aeschylus's *Oresteia*, and though Wagner had generous words to say about Shakespeare, the only paternity he claimed and coveted—another family romance—was that of Beethoven. Music drama understands itself as the ultimate realization—the *Aufhebung*, to deploy the Hegelian term—of absolute music. And "absolute music," with reference to Beethoven, is a term that Wagner invented. In this context, words and their sounds, down to the sounds of individual consonants, become musical atoms. Wagner's rhyme schemes in the *Ring* emerge out of one of his false philological genealogies from medieval German: so-called *Stabreim*, or consonantal alliteration at the start of the word (*Anfangslaute*), as opposed to the end-rhyme scheme (*Endreim*) of more standard poetic practice. Mellifluous consonants and their lyrical sounds—Wagner is especially fond of the soft *w*'s and *l*'s—are awarded to favored personalities (Siegmund, for example), whereas the hard sounds (hard *g*'s and *k*'s) begin the words of ugly characters (Alberich, Mime). Thus the ambivalent dialectic of music and drama, of music drama.

5. Between Knowing and Being

Wagnerian ambivalence, its moving pendulum of insight and ideology, involves also the pendulum between knowing and being. Marking divergent ways of finding a subject's place in the world, the knowing/being dialectic is key to the emergence of modernity as a mode of consciousness in general. It has peculiar potency in the German world, where it also posits musical form, experience, and argument in close orbit with political experience and philosophical argument.

Knowing assumes an action with two positions: the act of knowing and that of being known. Being assumes—or desires—a single position, the indivisibility of knower and known, or subject and object, self and other, self and world. We tend to understand this dualism as a philosophical issue, as indeed it is. Here, however, the history of philosophy merges with both the emergence of modern European politics and modern German music—music drama, in Wagner's case.[9] There is some heft to the old joke that "due to inclement weather, the revolution in Germany was held in music."

The energy of what we call modern—in history, philosophy, and art, and as a period, style, or claim—involves the displacement of being by knowing. In Europe, this displacement accompanies political and religious upheavals. In the period we now call "early modern," roughly 1500–1800, new forms of power, authority, and governance require legitimation through the fragile structures and human arguments of politics. Old regimes (which persist during this period even as they are embattled) are obliged constitutionally neither to examine nor to know neither themselves or the world over which they have sovereignty. They do not have to earn legitimacy, do not require the right to their sovereignty; they simply have it. Thus, they simply *are* in the world as sovereign powers. Monarchic offices as bearers of such sovereignty see themselves as earthly manifestations of divine power (which requires no legitimation). This is the principle of divine right in the European political tradition. The simultaneity of the political and scientific upheavals of this traditional world of sovereign being in seventeenth-century Europe is not accidental. The conception of the world as a terrain that must be examined and known without preconditions (via the modes of questioning that become the natural and the social sciences) also impacts the political world, with its newly open and constructed bases for authority. (In the English-language reception of traditional German political categories there is an ongoing debate about the optimal translation of the word *Herrschaft*: between domination, in other words a predicament in which the legitimation of authority is either irrelevant or suppressed, and sovereignty, where legitimation is relevant and possibly negotiable.) The seventeenth-century revolutions in science and politics rest in turn on the European destabilizations of the sixteenth-century Reformation, which produced a cognitive split and trauma in what had been accepted as the universal doctrine of a universal ("catholic") Church.

If, in pre-Reformation Christian Europe, the sovereign simply *was* sovereign—in other words, he held the right to divine rule without requiring the right—the system of a universal catholic faith allowed all faithful to share a small corner of that state of being which the sovereign grounded. Being-in-the-world, to seize on the twentieth-century terminology of Heidegger, which attempts precisely to recapture that religious state of being from the vantage point of twentieth-century philosophy, is thus a right and relic not only of the religious world, but of the undifferentiated religious world.

It is worth noting here, if only parenthetically, that Wagner had significant interest in this world and its loss through the Reformation. Wagner was himself a Protestant, born in the largely Lutheran kingdom of Saxony and city of Leipzig. The music dramas that engage explicitly Christian worlds and themes take place either in the pre-Reformation historical world (*Lohengrin*'s Antwerp), or in a mythic medieval landscape (*Tannhäuser*'s Thuringia, *Parsifal*'s Monsalvat). Nevertheless, *Lohengrin* reveals significant sensitivity to proto-Reformational conflicts. Henry the Fowler, the German king, visits the region along the Scheldt River to recruit mercenaries and believers to fight the Hungarians. From a mid-nineteenth-century German Protestant perspective, this set-up adds up to a premonition of the regional and religious wars of divided sixteenth-century Europe. Audiences may well have recognized in Lohengrin's swan a principal symbol of Martin Luther himself and the coming of the Reformation.[10]

Only *Die Meistersinger* takes place in the historical, biographical world of sixteenth-century Nuremberg. Though the specific terms of religious violence go unmentioned, cultural divisions and urban violence are both palpable and essential to its plot. As a comedy of reconciliation, it leads its hero, the cobbler and songster Hans Sachs, to reconcile aesthetic battles and, by implication, religious ones as well. Wagner's Sachs thus becomes the archetype of the nineteenth-century nationalist who will seek cultural and political unity out from the increasingly repressed reality of religious bifurcation (*Zwiespalt*).

The trauma of religious schism in sixteenth-century Europe cannot be overestimated. In a climate where unbelief, as the great historian Lucien Febvre argued in the 1930s, was cognitively impossible (another example of the potential cognitive violence of dividing by zero), the Solomonic crisis of authority and legitimacy between the two sides of the schism threatened eternal damnation for the soul of anyone who made the wrong decision. Sovereigns themselves were not spared this anxiety.[11] Though the problem spread across Europe and the New World, it was most severe in Germany. Germany remained the preeminent theater of religious warfare, the most scorched land of the Thirty Years' War (1618–48), which can be considered the "world war" of the seventeenth century. Even more important, the wave that divided the German world evenly between Catholics and Protestants has never receded, even though its force has been dulled by the long process of secularization. In nineteenth-century Germany, the cultural need for as well as the result of nationalism was the binding of Germans across religious divides. Since German historical scholarship is largely the result of the founding historians of the nineteenth century, German historiography's service to this nationalizing priority has never gone away, rendering any analysis of religious difference (including its displacement onto cultural terrain in the aftermath of secularization) difficult to uncover.

Life in a divided culture has countless results, beginning with the very perception of such division as a reality principle. The cultural Other must be contended with, must somehow be known. The condition of being, which amounts to the blending in of the self with the world in a condition of un-differentiation, is not possible. As soon as knowing—or perhaps, rather, *not* knowing—takes over, which happens at the moment of language, drama, and personification, the nostalgia for being, for undifferentiation and unity, emerges as well. The nostalgia for being quickly morphs into its more dangerous variant, namely the ideology of being, in other words the will to restore it. This is the will, essentially a political will, to save the world from difference.

The displacement of being by knowing tracks closely the displacement of religion by science. The standard term for this process is secularization. The corrective, however, to the standard and outdated paradigm of secularization lies in the term "displacement," rather than "replacement." In displacement, the earlier category remains present and active. If secularization involves the displacement of being, being's return is always a present force. The forms of historical understanding that understanding history as a clean march of progress—the national discourses in German, so-called Whiggish historiography in the British context, and the "evolution of liberal democracy" model that dominated U.S. discourse until at least the 1970s—assumed that every past disappeared once a present was staked out. Historical progress was emancipatory, asserting freedom from the past rather than the past's survival as a dimension, whether consoling or threatening, of the present. The survival of the past in the present presents a significant complication to all forms of periodization. The "past that does not go away" becomes another Other of the present. This mode of temporal double consciousness has been recognized slowly by historians following its pioneering theorization in psychoanalysis. Epochs, like persons, strive to get over their pasts as well as to hold on to them. In the psychoanalytic understanding of the person, the traumas of the past reside in the unconscious, whose contact is unavailable to the conscious self for the very protection of that self. If the past is an Other, then those aspects of my own self that are the products and results of the past (my own personal past as well as the cultural past) can constitute areas or dimensions of my own self that are Other or irreconcilable to me. The more intense the cultural climate of differentiation and conflict, the more vexed the content of the unconscious. We will come back to this in chapter 4, in the context of *Götterdämmerung*, in the context of a comparison of the unconscious as a cultural phenomenon in Germany (a highly differentiated culturescape) and Italy (a significantly less differentiated one).

Nostalgia for an undifferentiated world becomes a basic modern affect—or even a diagnosis. Nostalgia began, Svetlana Boym has shown, as a seventeenth-century diagnosis of a pathology.[12] We now accept it as a basic emotion. The nostalgia for undifferentiation is the desire for knowing to return to being, to oneness with the world, whether the natural world before culture (the founding trope of Jean-Jacques Rousseau's political theory, prior to the necessity of the social contract) or the Edenic or other cultural world prior to human conflict. No modern ideologies have proved more powerful than those claiming to deliver on the desired return to undifferentiation, on the promise to return from the state of knowing (and its essential partner, unknowing) to the state of being.

The challenge to psychoanalysis as a science of self- and world knowledge through the later twentieth century alongside the return to ideals of being, now understood according to categories such as identity or identity politics, involves the desire for a return to an undifferentiated self. Undifferentiation or, better, the denial of difference proves a close cognate of totalization, which in political terms becomes totalitarianism. Hence the ideology of totalizing political and religious movements and systems such as fascism, fundamentalism, and racism. In liberal, capitalist contexts, the rejection of psychoanalysis, that is, of the science of the self, and the disavowal of the differentiated self involves the rejection of too much work, too much time, too much expense, and the totalization of the self as the consumer. The consumer-as-self finds that self only within the objects of desire. Meet Fafner (chapter 3).

The differentiation between self and Other (whether the Other is a cultural Other, another person, or "the self as an Other"), between self and world, between a subject position and an object (or another subject) position, claims the central attention of the heyday of classical German philosophy: the half century of German idealism from the publication of Immanuel Kant's *Critique of Pure Reason* in 1781 to the death of Hegel in 1831. This is a turbulent period, but one during which German central Europe remains on its own tracks, at a significant distance from the trajectories of political revolution and reaction in France and of industrial revolution in England. The location of German power and culture shifts decidedly during these years from Austria to Prussia, from Vienna to Berlin. The rise of Prussia rests on two institutional and ideological foundations: the military and Protestant thought, including the latter's new and increasingly secular articulations. The poets and philosophers who came of age between the 1770s and the 1790s, a stunning demographic as well as cultural proliferation, were almost all the sons of pastors. Their largest institutional project took shape as the research university, exemplified by the University of Berlin, founded in 1810. They constitute a microcosm of the making of secular forms as displaced religious convictions.

Composers are rarely philosophers, and Wagner was certainly not one, despite his flirtation with the texts of Schopenhauer in the 1850s and his charismatic hold over the young Nietzsche in the 1860s. The connections between philosophy and music in Germany reside rather in their shared precedent of secularizing Protestant thinking. From the initial principle of the radical unknowability of God, as developed and intensified from Luther to Calvin, developed the understanding of the otherness of the world. Self and other, self and world thus always occupied two positions. Knowledge meant knowledge of the other position—including, eventually, the self as Other. Being, or the resolution of this dialectic, had lost legitimacy as a modern option.

The initial argument of Kant's *Critique of Pure Reason* was the grounding of the capacity of knowledge of an Other—the "synthetic a priori," in his jargon—in the internal (hardwired, we might say today) capacity of the mind. This basic paradigm remains largely in place today. But it is Hegel who challenged it fundamentally, indeed even traumatically. Kant's model of the mind and its relation to the world outside it is structural. Hegel replaces structure with history. For Hegel, the human mind evolves through the history of the world with a unified momentum that comes to embody the evolution and realization of human freedom. The human mind and world history are thus unified in the work of history, which is identical to the making of human freedom. In this respect, self and world are fused: not as Being, but rather as Becoming. Difference, displaced from a problem of structure to one of history, is no longer that between subject and object, me and you, one culture and another, but between one historical moment of a first-person subject—the "I" that speaks for the historical moment—and the same subject at a point in the future—the "I" that will be. For any individual or atomic "I"—the individual, the nation, the language, the religion—to have significance at all, the light of history must be shining on it; it must be in sync with world history as the unfolding of freedom.

The political ramifications of this Hegelian move have received voluminous attention without stable resolution. If the realization of world history is the perfection of human freedom, then the realization of freedom is identical to the "end of history." For Hegel, that dual goal was almost achieved by the French Revolution of 1789, until it was overtaken and delegitimated by the violence of the Terror of 1793-94. His next candidate for the achievement of the end of history was the Prussian state that employed him, though the scholars who argue for the preservation of his radical political edge hold that he was disenchanted with the reality of Prussian politics after 1815. In any case he did not live to see the conservative retrenchment of the Prussian monarchy and state in the 1830s and 1840s, culminating in the rejection of the liberal constitution proposed in Frankfurt in 1848. Following the defeat of 1848, German liberalism reconstituted itself at least in part on the basis of what became known as neo-Kantianism, in other words on the philosophical and political insistence on the subject-object, self-world distinction as the ethical basis of the relation of political power to the world it was supposed to serve. Pre-1848 German liberalism ceded to neo-Kantianism the principle of the Other as another, a depoliticization that made possible the significant shift of the liberal nationalism of 1848 to the national liberalism of 1870.

Neo-Kantianism held significant authority in German academic philosophy from the 1850s through the 1920s, despite its assault from Nietzsche at the beginning of its run and from Heidegger at the end. Heidegger's philosophical knockout of Ernst Cassirer in the legendary Davos debate of 1929 sealed neo-Kantianism's fate to philosophical posterity as somehow weak and doomed. But this judgment is unfair. The insistence on a double position of subject and object carries a basic political as well as ethical principle, which was taken up later, without reference to genealogy, by the discourses of the Other from Emmanuel Levinas to postcolonial theory. The responsibilities of knowing remain distinct from the pleasures of being and the latter's offer of subject-object, self-world reconciliation.

The formal capacities of music enabled it to enter this set of problems with uncanny presence. Music develops in time; there is no music that doesn't. (The image does not unfold through a designated period of time, though it demands time from the viewer. Aby Warburg and his practice of the cultural history of the image can be understood to invest an implied temporality in the image. For this reason his arguments have come to be of increasing interest in the study of cinema, which he did not address.) How deliberately, forcefully, and inexorably music marks and measures the passage of time in the articulation of its own forms as well as in the perception of its listeners informs the unlimited variety of musical works. German music in the fifty years of German idealism accrues new power and urgency as a music of becoming. This principle reaches its utmost intensity in Beethoven, and in those aspects of Beethoven which Wagner claimed as his model.

Becoming what? What, in other words, is the goal of a musical work such as a Beethoven symphony, its achievement as it reaches the end? A formalist and basically valid consideration of the question would involve the harmonic and rhythmic rules, formulas, and complications that the work engages and finally resolves. When the music is over, however, there is nothing. The end of its history is not the Prussian state; it is silence. The silence at the end of a musical performance, as conductors will attest and, even more, strive to produce, is not empty. It is a filled moment of time and space. It suggests a lived life as a realization of something, allowing the musical work and performance to reach completion in the form of an achievement. The existential analog to postmusical silence is death, but a death which retroactively foregrounds the music as the traversal of a meaningful, efficacious life. The texture and energy of the music's trajectory through its life is the struggle for knowledge, of the (musical) subject's knowledge of itself and its world. Music's analogy to human predicaments involves the articulation of the desire for knowledge along with the incapacity for absolute or certain knowledge. Nineteenth-century musical language, Wagner's above all, increases the scale of this challenge (some would say bloats it) to a saturation point. The early twentieth-century break into what is commonly called atonality emerges from the assertion that music's cognitive claims had become too easy, the musical narrative of human life (such as that in *Ein Heldenleben*) too glib.

The final words of another masterpiece that took a career to complete, Goethe's *Faust* (Part 2), clinch the impossibility of human knowledge at the end of the human life that strives for just that. Heavenly voices intone:

> Alles Vergängliche
> ist nur ein Gleichnis;
> das Unzulängliche,
> hier wird's Ereignis;
> das Unbeschreibliche,
> hier ist es getan;
> das Ewigweibliche
> zieht uns hinan.
>
> Everything transitory
> Is merely metaphor
> The unattainable
> Becomes here reality

> The indescribable
> Is here accomplished
> The eternal feminine
> Draw us on high.

Goethe's verses served the nineteenth century as a mantra for Romantic modernism and its principle, inherited from Protestant sources, of the unknowability of the absolute. In the same orbit, Wagner's music unfolds through an intricate discourse—musically, formally conceived—of knowledge, the desire for knowledge, and finally the impossibility of definitive knowledge. This is its modern and secular momentum. At the same time, Wagner's system-building can stray into overconfidence: the overconfidence of systematic thinking in its alleged grasp of the world. Music, as Gustav Mahler well knew when he set these words of Goethe to music at the end of his Eighth Symphony, doubles the argument by the very incapacity of its formal constitution to grasp hold of the world through signification, as language is able to do.

6. Getting It

Above I sketched the relative ambivalence of music and the sounds of words and their leading consonants as generators of music and drama in Wagner's aesthetic. This ambivalence begins to address the heightened claim of Wagner's music forms to signify dramatically, and to signify *tout court*. The claim and the ambivalence both intensify with the musical-dramatic practice that becomes the bedrock of Wagner's composition as well as the scholarly and popular treatments of it. This is the Wagnerian leitmotif, or signature tune, in Anna Russell's immortal and, as always, devastatingly accurate rendition. And what an unstable layer of bedrock it is!

The term "leitmotif" is not Wagner's but that of his acolyte and biographer Hans von Wolzogen. Von Wolzogen arrived in Bayreuth in 1877 to edit the journal *Bayreuther Blätter*, which he did until his death in 1938, by which time he had lived long enough to make several serious errors, including membership in the Nazi Party in 1933 and adherence to the racist mythology of Alfred Rosenberg. His first "thematic guidebook" appeared following the inaugural Bayreuth Festival and focused on the *Ring*; guides to *Tristan* and *Parsifal* followed in 1880 and 1882. His own Wagnerism was fanatically positivistic, a tendency that led him to work out the labeling and systematizing of the leitmotivic system that still controls much Wagnerism today—including much scholarship and almost all lay competence—and which some recent scholarship has only recently begun to dislodge. (Audiences of the Barenboim-Cassiers *Ring* at La Scala were invited to purchase a two-volume program book containing the full texts of the operas, beside which the full alleged system of leitmotifs is indicated, for better or worse, in color-coded luxury.)

The Will to Label is appealing and not irrational. The first and most basic music to form leitmotivic status in the opening moments of *Das Rheingold* possesses an unquestionable mimetic authority; formed out of the E-flat major chord that opens the cycle, its upward thrust is easily associated with the Rhine and its currents as metaphors of the repetitive rhythms of nature in time. This mimetic authority retains some of its magnetism when associations both structural and dramatic are built: the repeated upward-moving arpeggio that signifies the well-being of an unspoiled nature is thus answered, over the course of the four *Ring* operas, by an analogous descending arpeggio associated with anti-natural elements involving the gods, their imposed laws and contracts (Wotan's spear), and their demise. However, equally arresting and important leitmotifs seem to identify objects and ideas that lie beyond any mimetic capacity. Most fundamental and most unstable in this category, to my ear, is the motif identified with Nothung, the sword that Wotan fashions for Siegmund. Taking the musical form of another basic broken major chord, though partially inverted into the sequence 5-1-1(octave below)-3-5-1-3, this phrase cannot of course mimetically signify "sword" the way the first one can signify "river." More important, the fixing of this phrase as the label of a static object sucks much of the musical and dramatic energy and emotion out of its long life through the course of the *Ring*.

The so-called sword motif appears for the first time in an isolated C major clarion trumpet call in scene 4 of *Das Rheingold*, just before Wotan greets his new castle Valhalla prior to moving in with the family. The trumpet call and the phrase enter the moment as some kind of event, to be sure. Looking back from later points in the *Ring*, and depending on how the moment itself is staged and performed, we can reasonably associate the event with some kind of idea that enters Wotan's head at this instant. Having lost Alberich's ring to Fafner, the idea of regaining it through the actions of an unborn son may be occurring to him, and, quick thinker that he is, he may indeed be figuring out the plot by which to lodge a sword in a tree for that son—whom Wotan will by then have nurtured and abandoned—to find and extract by virtue of his own physical and erotic authority. Congratulations, an acerbic critic in the mold of Adorno would say: you have done your homework; you are listening by numbers. "Sword!" the La Scala libretto confirms!

Adorno famously ridiculed Wagner's composing-by-leitmotif as an instrument of his listener's self-flattery according to the pleasure of recognition and orientation through the four long evenings of the *Ring*. But Adorno may have attacked the wrong enemy if his own error here was to accept the nomenclature and signifying practice as laid out in von Wolzogen's catalog. Why should this clarion chord be heard statically to signify "sword"? Why not hear it through time and variation, first as a broken chord—a structure stretched into a moment of time and history—that does not signify or imitate and thus remains opaque as a musical dramatic figure and event, then slowly to take form as a projection of Wotan's desire, his will to knowledge as inspired by Erda, slowly then to accompany the vexed and tragic story of his paternity, Siegmund's abandonment and longing for his father, and so on? As the phrase lives its life, it loses its label.

In the developing dramatic action in scene 4 of *Das Rheingold*, the intrusion of the sword motif possesses a radical externality. We experience an undefined pleasure deriving from the basic musical grammar and sound of the major triad 5-1-1-3-5-1-3. We recognize the clarity of the musical utterance in grammatical, harmonic, and formal terms. If we are familiar with the subsequent history of this leitmotif and with the continuing plot of the *Ring*, we then have the choice of hearing from the future, retroactively from *Die Walküre* and beyond, or not. If we inhabit the moment without hearing backward from the future, we confront a seductive moment of musical opacity. The radical externality and opacity of the first announcement of the sword motif can be heard as analogous to the opening chords of Mozart's *Don Giovanni*, which we later learn to associate with the Commendatore and his ghost. At first, however, we appear in both cases to be hearing the orchestra shouting out the first thing that has entered its mind, to flag Joseph Kerman's legendary invective against the final moments of Puccini's *Tosca*, invoking it however as a mode of praise rather than insult. (Kerman's abiding 1957 classic *Opera as Drama* brought to opera in general both a Wagnerian aesthetic—the book's title is a clear riff on Wagner's three-volume manifesto *Opera and Drama* of 1852—along with a Wolzogenesque understanding of how leitmotifs work.) When the sword motif announces itself, we are drawn into the moment by its musical force, and we have learned enough about Wagner's musical idiom to know that some meaning will or at least *wants* to attach itself to the phrase, but we don't know what that meaning is. On the basis of this paradigmatic case (there are many others), we might therefore understand the general paradigm of the leitmotif—individual utterance and aesthetic system—as a trope of desire: the desire, constituted in music, to know and to signify, rather than the achievement or performance of either.

"What does 'to mean' mean?" asks Claude Lévi-Strauss; "It seems to me that the only answer we can give is that 'to mean' means the ability of any kind of data to be translated into a different language. I do not mean a different language like French or German, but different words on a different level."[13]

The sword motif returns with generous musical development in act 1, scene 2 of *Die Walküre* as Siegmund, in mortal danger, recollects a promise made by his lost father: "Ein Schwert verhiess mir der Vater" (Father promised me a sword). This phrase carries music in a major mode; the following phrase—"ich fänd' es in höchster Not" (I should find it at the moment of gravest danger) modulates suddenly to the minor mode. The major mode modulating to minor accompanies the mood shift from faith to fear. As Siegmund recollects the promise, the sword motif emerges, as we heard it in *Rheingold*; only now it is clearly identified, corroborated by the words. Once identified, it seems to play with itself, not evolving harmonically or structurally but becoming lyrical in its repetitions, as if a projection of paternal protection becomes a fantasy of paternal care, of paternal authority in the service of fatherly love. The music seems almost to caress itself, as a parent consoles a child—or as the child craves consolation. All of these references are sung by the trumpet in melancholy dialogue with the other instruments, with Siegmund, with the audience.

The celebrated E-flat major arpeggios that get the opening of *Das Rheingold* under way come convincingly close to embodying the pulse of the Rhine. The music also produces waves, surges, rhythms, repetitions. It can indeed almost be the river. But this is on the level of a child's costume party: "Who am I?" asks the child in reference to a costume or temporary disguise. More compelling is the fact that music cannot know the river, just as culture cannot know nature.

On this point we can listen to the director Ruth Berghaus, who gave a series of interviews in connection with her *Ring* (1985–87) for the Frankfurt Opera. Her point is the gap between art and nature. Art can say something about nature, she insists, but art cannot know nature. For this reason, a stage set cannot approximate nature—and shouldn't try to. Musical notes, she says, are not part of nature. A scrupulous student of Wagner's scores, including his obsessively detailed scenic descriptions and stage directions,

Berghaus remains mystified by his opening directive, "Der Rhein fliesst von rechts nach links" (The Rhine flows from right to left). What can this mean? she asks. "Das Wasser hat so viel mit der Natur zu tun als eine Note zu tun hat" (The water has just as much to do with nature as a musical note does), she says.[14] Berghaus lightly touches here on a dual dialectic: art and culture cannot know nature; music cannot know the world or articulate its connection to the world as language can.

We grasp here a basic principle about aesthetic knowledge, or the kind of knowledge that art makes possible. The principle coalesces most in music, as a mode of art that can know but cannot speak. Music knows the world and cannot know the world. Musical knowledge involves its knowing that it cannot know the world. This is where the capacities and paradoxes of art become essential to the understanding of what knowledge is and how it works. Also, this is where art's cognitive rigor and modesty meet political responsibility. The world remains other, never to be subsumed or spoken for.

Adam Phillips has explored this cognitive and political paradox through a wonderful disquisition on the expression "getting it." The argument is linguistic, psychoanalytic, and political. "Getting it" is always paired with "not getting it," as in getting or not getting a joke, understanding or not understanding, being included in a community of reference or being excluded from it. You have to "get it" to be able to live in the world: turn on the computer, feed the baby, and so on. Phillips's argument takes off, however, in his valuation of *not* getting it. Aesthetic and psychoanalytic education, he argues, should pay attention to the dynamics of not getting it, should teach "how not to ride a bike." The world, like the unconscious, remains a zone of unknowability, the recognition of which makes knowledge possible. "So we might consider," he writes,

> what it would be to live a life in which getting it is not always the point, in which there is nothing, to all intents and purposes, to get; and our picture of this can be, in adult life, when we are lost in thought, absorbed in something without needing to know why we are absorbed, or indeed what we are absorbed in; or when we dream. Or going back to the life of the infant, the life before jokes, before language, which is a life sponsored by somebody who has to be able to get it, that is, to imagine the baby's needs, to imagine what will assuage the infant's distress.[15]

Phillips highlights the political stakes of the issue when he writes: "Knowing other people, in psychoanalytic language, can be a defense, the defense, against acknowledging their actual existence, and what we need their existence for."[16]

Like Winnicott, whose biography he wrote, as well as Ernest Jones and Freud, Phillips is sensitive to the cultural and ideological contexts of Being as a state of prelapsarian grace, unity, and sacredness. States of being are compromised—or succeeded, in historical terms—by the reality principles of knowing and doing. For Freud and Jones, this original state of grace is imagined as the unity of infant and mother, to be lost through the traversal of the Oedipal crisis. "What if," Phillips asks,

> say, that Oedipal crisis—as described by Freud and Jones's Hamlet— killed off the possibility of being, made it impossible; that like a secular Fall it, irredeemably, put being and doing at odds with each other; 'contaminated' them, to use Winnicott's word. Perhaps, Winnicott is suggesting, the tragedy of the Oedipus complex ineluctably dissociates being from doing. In this sense, one might say, Hamlet doesn't want to—can't bear to—think of an alternative to being; the possibility of being has already been lost. There is only doing for him now.[17]

The being/doing duality, possibly more than the being/knowing one, can easily be gendered, which is in fact how Winnicott treated it with reference to Freud and the question of bisexuality. A 1966 essay on *Hamlet* sets out with a section called "The Male and Female Elements Contrasted," where Winnicott writes that the female element "has nothing to do with drive (or instinct) ... it leads us to *being*, and this forms the only basis for self-discovery and a sense of existing ... when the girl element in the boy or girl baby finds the breast it is the self that has been found. If the question is asked, what does the girl baby do with the breast?, the answer must be that this girl element is the breast." In Phillips's summary, "Winnicott *seems* to be trying to describe two attitudes, two ways or relating to an object, that exist in sequence: first being, then doing. One can *be* the object—Winnicott likens this to primary identification—or one can do something to it; one can be absorbed, immersed or one can use for some purpose." Phillips amends the model with the comment that the two states *"don't need to be gendered, perhaps, to be of interest."* He says also that psychoanalytic theory "is all about doing." He would probably not object to the argument that psychoanalysis as both theory and therapy is about knowing (of self and world) and doing, and about the necessity to leave behind being beyond such refractory flashes as can be provided by aesthetics and sensuality, art and sex.

In the *Ring*, knowing/being and doing/being relate closely to another duality that is basic to the *Ring* and that has been considered by some of the strongest recent scholarship. This is the duality of action (the Being of drama) and narration (the Knowing of drama).

Recall that Wagner sketched and wrote the texts to the *Ring* in reverse order, beginning with the story of Siegfried's death. The increasing need for and heft of the backstory produced the three preceding works, which Wagner then composed in forward order. As the tetralogy's text evolved, he still wished to maintain the priority of the denouement. The original idea of the action-opera supported by a long, indeed ever lengthening setup continued to dominate the explicit aesthetic—musical and dramatic—of the entire final tetralogy. This aesthetic gives priority to action over narration. Yet the *Ring*'s evolution displays a persistent overtaking of structure by scaffold. *Das Rheingold*, *Die Walküre*, and *Siegfried* are as definitively important as *Götterdämmerung*. And the cycle's narrations, from Loge's in *Das Rheingold* to Brünnhilde's at the end of *Götterdämmerung*, equal and perhaps overtake the action scenes for their depth and subtlety of musical form and portrayed human complexity.

Carolyn Abbate has described the action/narration paradox as the "great paradox in the *Ring*'s history, and what many consider to be the great flaw in its text: that the narratives, despite Wagner's glee over their elimination, were kept."[18] It is not clear who these "many" are, as serious listeners come quickly to prize the narrations, even and most especially the mother of all monologues—Wotan's at the cycle's turning point in the second act of *Die Walküre*. Wagner himself appears to have reversed his principle as early as 1852 when, having completed the prose poems of the four works, he expanded existing narrations and added more. Wagner himself "came to believe," as Abbate concludes, "that narrative—far from being made expendable by the expansion of *Walküre* and *Rheingold*—was, after all, crucial to the kind of work that he had conceived." Indeed, it is often the retention of action as the necessary representation of plot business that slows down the works, beginning with scene 1 of *Rheingold* and the apparent necessity of all three Rhinemaidens to get through their feigned seductions of Alberich. It's the narratives, beginning with Loge's splendid one in scene 2 of *Rheingold*, that bring history and dramatic depth to the characters and their plots. Both we the listeners and Wagner are more convinced, it seems, by representations of knowing than by those of being. By the time he gets to *Parsifal*, Wagner appears to have gained enough confidence to produce a series of scenes constructed on narrations alone. In *Tristan*, this tendency is occasionally compromised, such as in the penultimate scene of act 3 and the arrival of King Marke's ship with its excessive stage business and relatively weak music.

Wagner knew what the pioneering historians of his generation also knew and indeed codified: that history is a function of historiography, that history is, as Jakob Burckhardt asserted, "what one age finds of interest in another." On the one side: evidence. On the other: interest and possible distortion. Wagner's narrations cannot be tested by evidence. They can only be compared for their various distortions, rendering their tellings into rough cuts of a Freudian structure of narration as distorted projections of the origins of present moments.

I would suggest hearing the leitmotifs, individually as well as within their relations, webs, and sequences, as elements of narration and thereby of knowledge on the long spectrum of accuracy and distortion, truth and falsehood. The unstable authority of the leitmotifs themselves bespeaks the same status with regard both to the narrating characters and to the music dramas themselves. The sword motif hovers between a reference to the sword and, what is more interesting, a reference to the reference of the sword. The system of leitmotifs as a whole becomes a dense forest of musical inarticulacy and desire—the desire to speak and to signify. This will become one the qualities of the actual forest that accompanies the plot of the *Ring*, especially *Walküre* and *Siegfried*, an opaque realm that holds the biggest secrets and the biggest revelations. We might thus entertain an immediate revision or complication of my proposal in this paragraph: namely, that we understand the phenomenological experience of leitmotif as a force field of knowing and being, distance and absorption, outside and inside—the unstable meeting point of action and narration. It is a musical act (speech act) in the present, as well as a reference to the past, to story and history.

Not surprisingly, Wagner himself instructs us on how (not) to get what he is doing through the words of the cobbler poet Hans Sachs, one half of his alter ego, commenting on his first impression of the young poet Walther von Stolzing, its other half:

> Und doch, 's will halt nicht geh'n:
> Ich fühl's und kann's nicht versteh'n: —

kann's nicht behalten, — doch auch nicht vergessen:
und fass' ich es ganz, kann ich's nicht messen!

And yet it just won't go.
I feel it, and can't understand it;
can't hold on to it — but can't forget it;
I think I've got it, then can't figure it out!

7. Songlines

The sequences and webs of leitmotifs do indeed form the momentum and arguments of Wagner's soundscape, his unending melody. I would hazard describing together these elements of the Wagnerian soundscape — leitmotif, argument, momentum — as Wagner's songlines. *Songlines* is the title of Bruce Chatwin's celebrated personal ethnography of aboriginal culture in Australia. Modernism, as Hermann Broch argued, involves primarily the impossible attempt to recapture the primal cultural and cognitive state of myth:[19]

> Aboriginals, it was true, could not imagine territory as a block of land hemmed in by frontiers: but rather as an interlocking network of "lines" or "ways through."
>
> "All our words for 'country,'" he said, "are the same as the words for 'line.'"
>
> For this there was one simple explanation. Most of Outback Australia was arid scrub or desert where rainfall was always patchy and where one year of plenty might be followed by seven years of lean. To move in such landscape was survival: to stay in the same place suicide. The definition of a man's "own country" was "the place in which I do not have to ask." Yet to feel "at home" in that country depended on being able to leave it. Everyone hoped to have at least four "ways out," along which he could travel in a crisis. Every tribe — like it or not — had to cultivate relations with its neighbor.
>
> ...
>
> "All right," I nodded; "Are you saying that a trade route always runs along a Songline?"
>
> "The trade route *is* the Songline," said Flynn. "Because songs, not things, are the principal medium of exchange. Trading in 'things' is the secondary consequence of trading in song."

Before the whites came, he went on, no one in Australia was landless, since everyone inherited, as his or her private property, a stretch of the Ancestor's song and the stretch of country over which the song passed. A man's verses were his title deeds to territory. He could lend them to others. He could borrow other verses in return. The one thing he couldn't do was sell or get rid of them.[20]

If we can hear musical texture as a mode of self-disclosure to and engagement with the world, as desired meaning-making across the reaches of space and time of a vast soundscape (as the stand-in for landscape), we pay homage to the desire of music drama to operate at the level of myth. The paradox of modernism is its desire to embrace the "now" as well as the moment of unmediated origins: the origins of culture in myth. In this way, modernism is both self-aware and self-conscious (the two different English words translate a single German one: *selbstbewusst*), while desirous of integration into the fundamental being of the world. The songline integrates — as the ethnography and poetry of the songline can only *wish* to integrate — subject and object, analysis and absorption, conscious and unconscious, knowing and being. In a similar way, we can speculate, Kant's science of reason prefigures the science of the unconscious (namely, psychoanalysis), while Hegel's integrative model of spirit (*Geist*), as the engine of the world and history, prefigures the art of the unconscious (as acknowledged and respected by Freud) as well as the later integrative philosophies of being in their varieties from, say, Rosenzweig to Heidegger. That same integration was furiously resisted by Adorno, who called it reconciliation, called it false and dangerous, and, musical thinker that he was, pinned much of the blame for its seductiveness and toxicity on Wagner. Adorno may have been correct while also protesting too much, and therefore not recognizing the other side, the critical and self-critical side, of Wagner's art.

A vast music drama claiming to operate at the level of myth, the *Ring* is ultimately about human knowledge rendered inadequate and tragic by its own existential limitations and fallibilities. Brünnhilde's knowledge comes too late. That it is a tale told in music assures the formal instantiation of the human inability to attain full knowledge and its articulation — the conviction that human life remains fallible and limited in its place in the world. The question persists: does the *Ring* know itself to be part of that fallible world, or does it stray into ideology by thinking of itself as an exception? Is the *Ring* a closed system, indicative of mythology, or an open system, indicative of history?[21] Do the *Ring* and we devotees of it together want to know the world and its passions, or does it—do we—in listening to it and to the world, seek to *be* the world, to be at one with the world, uniting ourselves with it, the world and the earth, uniting our ears and minds with its body and ours, according to the world of myth and the myths of mindfulness?

ONE

History and the Stage

1. Impossible Origins

GOD CREATED THE UNIVERSE, WE READ, IN SIX DAYS. IN THE opening moments of *Das Rheingold*, Richard Wagner repeats the task in 136 bars. Both creation processes unfold through the same principle: the birth and proliferation of differentiation. In the biblical account, differentiation originates in the visual world (the separation of light from darkness) and proceeds to the material (the earth from the sky) and, finally, to the biological (species from species, in a sequence similar to the one that Charles Darwin would propose in the 1850s, the decade of *Das Rheingold*). The Wagnerian universe originates within a primal sound. We can choose to understand this first sound to be a low E-flat played by the double basses. But in the theater, the sound emerges *as* sound, and not yet as music, in a manner that precedes and defies classification. *Das Rheingold* opens in a mysterious transition from nothing to something, and no more. The music doesn't announce or even disclose its presence. This sonic event lasts long enough for us to know that what we hear and experience is not yet music, an effect unparalleled in musical experience. When the second sound emerges (a B-flat) we may already hear the interval of a major fifth and thus the harmonic relation most basic to Western music; we may already hear, in other words, the promise of music. The third note repeats the original E-flat an octave higher; the fourth—a G natural—supplies the third value in the major triad. This sequence repeats and increases its pulse and motion, adding rhythm (a musical value) as well as urgency, agency, and even desire. If we are good Wagnerians, if we learn our leitmotifs and continue to remind ourselves of them, we know that this music is supposed to represent nature and the Rhine. In a mid-nineteenth-century German context, the Rhine possesses mythical value as the alleged primal locus of the earth and of the world itself: the world before language and before meaning. National culture fuses myth with history, nature with culture. The transition to the world of language and meaning—to the human world—happens abruptly with the entrance of the First Rhinemaiden, and the disruption comes as a shock. Woglinde's first *words*—"Weia, Wage, Woges"—mean nothing; they momentarily extend the state of pure sound that the prelude has introduced. Proto-music (which by now has become music in its harmonic grammar and syntax) is now joined by proto-language. For Wagner, however, these protowords are in fact already musical sounds, as he had a special affection for the sound of the German *w*, as we will hear throughout the *Ring*. Woglinde's fourth and fifth words—"du Welle" (you wave)—break through into human language. At this point the *Ring*'s action gets under way, and for the listener, only minutes into this epic, four-work series, stretching over a week, and often materializing as productions in opera houses over several years—something is already over, something has already been lost: the state of nature; the world before time. It is as if we had suddenly been granted a momentary reentry into a sonic, cognitive Eden, into our own infancy, into consciousness before language. We only grasp the shape of this primitive cognitive experience when it is over, and we understand it through the melancholy of loss and ephemerality that informs all earthly reality. The *Rheingold* prelude in its ephemerality satisfies for another, related reason: it allegorizes the building of a perfect world, or rather a perfect microcosm, out of the construction of harmonious units. This simple utopian construction is limited to music alone, and to the simplest components of the European musical tradition. This act of creation cannot be sustained or expanded; it is what will never happen in the course of the *Ring*'s story, indeed what will never happen when music enters the world through language, personification, human life. Thus the primal energy unit, the first low E-flat that emerges from nothingness, is joined by the interval of the perfect fifth. We might think of the biblical version of this creation moment in which the differentiation of succession is confused with the differentiation of partnership: Adam to Eve; Adam and Eve. But the realities of personification and convention take over once such a story is in place. "Adam and Eve" is already a human complication, gendered, balanced/imbalanced, and so forth. The addition of the second basic note may be the *Ring*'s most perfect moment, even though—or, rather, precisely because—its story hasn't started yet, hasn't had to recognize and become part of, consistent with, worldly realities: time, negotiation, mortality, impurity, corruption. The E-flat simply receives a perfect sonic partner, and it will not happen again. In human terms, this involves a fantasy of intimacy as the perfect and impossible combination of sameness and otherness, a duplication of the self and the arrival of a perfect Other. Going forward, this proto-music produces the elements of a major triad by filling the interval of the fifth with a third and then the octave, forming what might be heard to allegorize both the nuclear family and the initiation of future generations, with the octave representing repetition with difference. Thus the harmonic units of the major chord—I-V-III-VIII—allegorize the birth of history and human kinships and communities from the birth of the nuclear family, just as Karl Marx imagined the dawn of human history in his early writings of the 1840s, shortly before Wagner began making his first sketches for the *Ring*.[1]

Now, there is a potential musicological or music-historical disagreement with my account of the birth of music from sound and from nothingness. This has to do with the specific pitch of the originating sounds in the double basses—an E-flat—and its succession by the E-flat major triad. In real terms, the sounding of the E-flat (to say nothing, obviously, of the enormous apparatus and practical world of the orchestra and the opera house) presupposes a musical language, and the triad introduces a known musical structure and grammar. In addition, the key of E-flat major held a distinct aura for Wagner and his ideological investments. To Wagner and his contemporaries, E-flat major and its sonorities signified a heroic sound and style, mostly because Beethoven appeared to invest it with that quality. E-flat major is the key of his Third Symphony (the *Eroica*) and of the *Emperor* Concerto, among other works. But even before Beethoven, the theorist Francesco Galeazzi had identified E-flat major as "a heroic key, extremely majestic, grave and serious."[2]

As for the apparatus of the orchestra and opera house, including the work of its laborers, this is what Wagner strove to hide from the audience's eyes and ears when he designed the Bayreuth Festival hall and stage. *Das Rheingold* and *Die Walküre* had their premieres in Munich (in 1869 and 1870 respectively), but the full *Ring* opened the theater that Wagner designed for his own festival in Bayreuth in 1876. Its raked stage and hidden orchestra pit provided a unique acoustic, throwing the orchestral sound to the stage so that it blended with the singers' voices before being returned into the hall. Even more fundamental was the ideology of this configuration: the claim of the hidden pit to bring the Bayreuth audience directly into the mythical world of the *Ring* while hiding from sight and mind the mediative apparatus of orchestra as well as stage machinery—in other words, by suppressing the means of production (pun intended). This gesture grounds Adorno's critique of Wagner generally. "Wagner's oeuvre," Adorno writes, "comes close to the consumer goods of the nineteenth century which knew no greater ambition than to conceal every sign of the work that went into them."[3]

For Adorno, the suppression of the means of production is fundamental to Wagner's sound world, his construction of the orchestra, and his highlighting of individual instruments as well as—most originally for Adorno—his building of instrument families, such as the clarinets in relation to the tubas. Adorno plays closest attention to the horns, the instrument and sound with the most direct relation to mythical soundscapes and landscapes associated with the forest and the hunt. The horn is the third instrument we hear in the opening bars of *Das Rheingold*, following the double bass and bassoon. The salient point here—the meeting point of the technical and the ideological—is that Wagner's writing for horn (including for multiple horns—eight are required for *Rheingold*) depends on the modern valve horn, developed during Wagner's youth, but exudes a nostalgia for the simple, unmediated and unpredictable sound of the natural (valveless) horn. For Adorno,

> Wagner, like the critics of political economy, was under no illusions about the price that had to be paid for progress. No one who has ever heard a natural horn and a valve-horn, one after the other, will be inclined to question where the "true character" of the horn whose loss he mourns is to be found. It is in the trace that lingers on the in the horn of the way in which the note has been produced. A note "sounds like a horn" as long as you can still hear that it has been played on the horn: its origin, together with the risk of a false note, help to form the quality of the sound. It is this trace that is lost in the valve-horn. Wagner's horns are often compared to the piano pedals ... the difference between the pedaled note and the non-pedaled note on the piano is that in the former the trace of its production, which is heard at the moment when the hammer strikes the string, is eliminated. Something of the same kind happens with the horns, since the use of the valve mechanism alienates them from the immediate production of their own sound.[4]

Think forward now to the young Siegfried's horn playing in the forest scene of in act 2 of *Siegfried*. Rejecting the natural horn he fashions from a twig, he finds the right sound—the dragon-awakening sound—in the real instrument he carries on his belt. Wagner gets the joke here—even at his own expense. The episode must be understood as a self-aware riff on the natural-versus-valve horn issue highlighted by Adorno.

As the action of *Das Rheingold* takes off, we are in a universe defined by music drama: by the specifically Wagnerian universe of music, text, and stage, in which language, meaning, and human drama itself all revert to the authority of music. Here Wagner stakes his claim as the only true heir to Beethoven, the only rightful inheritor of absolute music—the term, again, that Wagner himself invented. Wagner's claim is not to write program music, but its opposite: absolute music that is able to signify, and thus to fulfill, the promise announced in the final movement of Beethoven's Ninth Symphony. There as elsewhere, Beethoven composed not only music but the desire of music to speak. The radical exception of the Ninth Symphony lay in its transgression—in the context of symphonic form and principles—to break through into speech and words. To this transgression Wagner would add the stage and its visual world, all along claiming to extend the reach and the signifying potential of the Beethovenian symphony, claiming as well never to participate in the groundless and gravity-free world of Italian opera.

2. History and the Stage

What kind of human world are we in, as *Das Rheingold* proceeds with Alberich's theft of the gold? The increasing pulse of the Rhine in the prelude's world of nature is now personified into the varieties of human desire that will dominate and determine the *Ring*'s plot. The *Ring* explores human desire, or, rather, human will, to use the Schopenhauerian word to which Wagner and his texts became ever more susceptible. The *Ring*'s first desire is lust—Alberich's for the Rhinemaidens. They, more respectably, refer to love. Alberich displaces his lust into a will to power, the desire he will share with Wotan (who, however, does not give up on lust). Wotan's third mode of desire, as inspired by Erda, is the will to knowledge. He will bequeath this mode of desire to his daughter Brünnhilde; in achieving knowledge, she will end the story. The human world of the *Ring*, then, examines these three patterns of human desire: lust/love, power, and knowledge.

A more precise picture of the human world of the *Ring* must depend on staging. Here, the history of *Das Rheingold* and the entire *Ring* onstage, from the premieres of 1869 (*Rheingold*) and 1876 (the full *Ring*) to the present, reveals some basic paradigms and some fundamental differences.

We might divide the history of the Wagner stage (with special emphasis on the *Ring*) into four historical and stylistic periods:

1. 1876–1944: mythistory
2. 1951–75: modernist myth
3. 1976–80: history
4. 1980s–: conservative myth

The first period, from 1876 (the Bayreuth premiere of the full cycle) to 1944 (the year of the closure of Bayreuth in the context of war and total mobilization) involves the sense of the abiding validity of the "original" Bayreuth style and production, as supervised by Wagner himself and with his own stage directions written into the score. This style also retains the claim of music drama, the *Ring*, and their theorists (including Nietzsche in *The Birth of Tragedy from the Spirit of Music* in 1871). That central claim is to reanimate the spirit of Greek tragedy as the modern *Gesamtkunstwerk:* capable not only of telling the national story, but of actually forming a national consciousness adequate to the moment of German national and imperial emergence in 1870–71. Thus, the "original" Wagner style involves the fusion of myth and history, in other words the claim to inhabit a new moment of national cultural foundation that is itself simultaneous with the ability to tell the story of the nation. This is a naive style (in Schiller's sense of the word); it contains no critical or self-critical perspective in relation to historical or other processes.

The reconstitution of German society after the Second World War and the "year zero" of 1945 in many ways found its core challenge in the politics of Bayreuth, which had served as a symbolic center of the Nazi regime. From its reopening in 1951, Bayreuth came to signify both the continuity of the past as well as the need for a total break from it. The break was announced from the stage by the so-called neo-Bayreuth style associated with Wieland Wagner. The composer's grandson had debuted as a set designer with *Parsifal* in 1938 and continued with *Die Meistersinger* in 1943–44 — the only production staged in Bayreuth during the later years of the war. Both stagings followed the Bayreuth naturalist tradition loyal to the original productions there, with the infamous exception involving the splicing of uniformed SS officers into *Die Meistersinger*'s festive final choral scene. All this vanished from Wieland's postwar style. Wieland's scenic style now offered a sleek visual modernism grounded in the fin-de-siècle innovations of Adolphe Appia, Alfred Roller, and others. Sets were minimal; lighting was emphasized, as were core symbols. Yet Wieland's revolution remained paradoxical in its combination of modernism with political safety, focusing on myth as a hedge against the engagement with history—Wagner's, the *Ring*'s, and Germany's. Since modernism involves a sense of the moment and thereby a sense of history, Wieland's style can be described as antimodernist just as much as modernist.

Myth engages the deepest structures of human experience: the invariant elements of life and history, as Claude Lévi-Strauss taught us, as distinct from the variants, which form the material of history: "Probably there is nothing more than that in the structuralist approach; it is the quest for the invariant, or for the invariant elements among superficial differences."[5] Myth without history (the latter of which the structuralist assertion relegates, at some political and human peril, to the level of the superficial difference) thus avoids history's specific traumas and crimes. Wieland Wagner's neomythic style found a scholarly correlative in the Jungian *Ring* analysis of Robert Donington.[6] Wieland's visual modernism was stunning and innovative. Without doubt it was visually challenging as well. But it was also fundamentally comforting, because the scenic removal of history, and of Wagner from history, allowed Bayreuth audiences (and their increasingly global counterparts) to disaggregate both Wagner and Wagner reception from the traumas and responsibilities of German—and, later, global—history.

For this reason, it turned out to be not Wieland Wagner in the 1950s but Patrice Chéreau in 1976 who generated the real postwar Wagner revolution, although this sea change, unlike the previous one, was not generated by a general political and human trauma. In his now legendary staging for the Bayreuth centennial, Chéreau recast the *Ring* as a historical epic of modern Germany from 1870 until around 1930, that is, from the moment of unification and empire to the Weimar crisis and the rise of Nazism and its path to cataclysm and genocide. Chéreau's scenic revolution found an essential partner in Pierre Boulez's conducting, which cleaned up, sharpened, and clarified the orchestral textures. Boulez's musical intervention amounted also to a direct and explicit historical correction, as the players were instructed (to their considerable irritation) not to produce the uniformly thick sound to which they had become accustomed. "Continent obstructed by fog" supposedly read a sign at London's prewar Victoria Station—a message about which postwar British philosophers loved to chuckle. Boulez cleared Bayreuth's orchestral fog, just as Chéreau cleared its scenic false clarity.

Chéreau and Richard Peduzzi, his scenic designer, put on the stage a historicist and materialist *Ring* that shocked its initial audiences but became a classic even to the Bayreuth audiences who initially rejected it. (The typical Bayreuth production run is five years; in its final year, 1980, the production, now acclaimed as a classic, was filmed for television.) Scene 1 of *Das Rheingold* opened on the site of a slowly rotating hydraulic dam. If this image seemed to betray the work's plot claim to develop out of a state of pure nature, it restored that possibility to the audience's imagination by rotating slowly and refracting shimmering effigies of leaves and water. Even more fundamentally and allegorically, the mesmerizing rotating dam functioned as a metonym for the *Ring*, for the very idea of cycles and circularity. And, as I argued above, once the opening of *Das Rheingold* reaches musical language and speech (in the Rhinemaidens' words), it has left a state of nature behind in any case. Here the Rhinemaidens were (likely) prostitutes and Alberich an unhappy dam or factory worker, a member of the mid-century industrial proletariat.

Chéreau's basic model was clearly George Bernard Shaw's 1898 essay *The Perfect Wagnerite: A Commentary on the Niblung's Ring*, which affirmed the story's place in the world of industrial capitalism and class conflict, the world of Marx and Engels as translated by Fabian socialism:

> The Ring, with all its gods and giants and dwarfs, its water-maidens and Valkyries, its wishing-cap, magic ring, enchanted sword, and miraculous treasure, is a drama of today, and not of a remote and fabulous antiquity.
>
> You can see the process for yourself in every civilized country today, where millions of people toil in want and disease to heap up more wealth for our Alberics, laying up nothing for themselves, except sometimes horrible and agonizing disease and the certainty of premature death. All this part of the story is frightfully real, frightfully present, frightfully modern; and its effects on our social life are so ghastly and ruinous that we no longer know enough of happiness to be discomposed by it.[7]

Chéreau of course acknowledged Shaw's text and model. So far as I know, he did not acknowledge a more recent analog: Joachim Herz's full *Ring* for Leipzig (1973–76), whose *Götterdämmerung* had premiered in March 1976, months before Chéreau's Bayreuth premiere.

Fitting with the social-realist preferences of the East German regime, Herz's *Ring* also offered an epic of industrial capitalism and its excesses.

Nibelheim became a steelworks plant, instantiating the so-called Second Industrial Revolution of the 1870s and its dominance by German steel and chemicals. Similarly, the hall of the Gibichungs in act 2, scene 1 of *Götterdämmerung* was rendered as a giant turbine hall (*Turbinenhalle*). Herz described the first act of *Die Walküre* as "in der gutbürgerlichen Wohnstube à la Ibsen" (a comfortable bourgeois sitting room à la Ibsen). He described his and Rudolf Heinrich's design for Valhalla as "stolen architecture," an effect they achieved through eclectic quotations of late nineteenth-century historicist public architecture: Brussels's Palais de Justice, the imperial staircase (Kaisertreppe) of the Vienna Burgtheater, Milan's Galleria, and the fierce, resentful Niederwalddenkmal—the post-1871 monument overlooking the Rhine and celebrating German unification following military victory against the "sworn enemy," France. It was certainly clear to Herz (who was also the Intendant of the Leipzig Opera), to Heinrich (based in Munich), and to much of their audience that all these source locations were forbidden destinations to East German citizens, just as Valhalla would have been beyond access to the non-gods of the story with whom the production sympathized.[8]

Chéreau's *Personenregie*—his building and direction of characters and their emotional states and gestures—was as inspired as his overall historical conception. Many of the gestures he developed with his singer-actors— especially the intense emotional bonds between characters, from the most erotic (Siegmund and Sieglinde) to the most violent (Wotan and Alberich, Wotan and Siegmund)—were retained in subsequent productions, even while the historical argument was given up in favor of a return to the default universe of myth. This return has largely dominated in the last thirty or so years, with a wide spectrum of visual and technical differentiation, to be sure, from the austerity of the work of Harry Kupfer and the five directors (Joachim Schlömer, Christoph Nel, Jossi Wieler/Sergio Morabito, and Peter Konwitschny) of the 1990s Stuttgart *Ring* and the repetition of that concept to open the new opera house in Toronto (2006); to the Walt Disney-like techno-atavistic kitsch of the Otto Schenk and Günther Schneider-Siemssen production at the Metropolitan Opera (1989–2009), to the visual burlesque of Achim Freyer's Los Angeles cycle, complete in 2010. For the run-up to the Wagner bicentennial, the Met replaced the fully nostalgic Schenk and Schneider-Siemssen production with Robert Lepage's more abstract and machine-driven version, dominated by a near proscenium-scaled rotating machine resembling a giant dental apparatus. In the end, however, Lepage's production proved more nostalgic than avant-garde, as it relied on conventional key props and naturalistic screen projections.

Chéreau's *Ring* was historical, or more accurately historicizing, in quite a literal way, as it proceeded in linear time, over the several generations from the *Gründerzeit* (the founders' decade or take-off period of the German Empire in the 1870s) to the late Weimar Republic period. These distinct eras evinced changing scenic styles, from the interior spaces and costumes of the Second Empire to the cinematic tableaux of the 1920s. Nineteenth-century scenes were painterly: Wotan's living room (seen in act 2 of *Die Walküre*) was also Ibsenesque, while Brünnhilde's rock offered an explicit quotation of Arnold Böcklin's *Isle of the Dead*. *Götterdämmerung* and the hall of the Gibichungs were all Fritz Lang and mass politics. Thus the Bayreuth public was asked to experience the epic of the *Ring* as the story of their own past, a past that was gone but that the present generation (as of 1976) still remembered well and for which it bore considerable responsibility. The anonymous crowd that survived the cataclysm of the twilight of the gods slowly stood up and faced not the ruins of Valhalla, as Wagner's stage directions prescribe, but, menacingly, the audience—the Bayreuth audience of 1976, that is, whom the directors implicitly accused of responsibility for Germany's catastrophe. This gesture, along with others, has often been repeated, if without the devastating historical, political, or emotional specificity with which the elite Bayreuth audience of 1976 was targeted.

Guy Cassiers's *Ring* introduced a completely new paradigm, a new confrontation of art and history. This new paradigm proved fundamentally consistent with Patrice Chéreau's insistence that the historical realities of the world be recognized in general and in Wagner's epic. "Wir können aus dieser Welt nicht fallen" (We cannot fall out of this world), to repeat a line from the playwright Friedrich Hebbel that Freud especially liked to quote. However, unlike the historical epic that Chéreau presented, Cassiers's *Ring* did not take place in a consistently articulated historical era, nor did it move through historical periods or generations chronologically. It did not begin in 1870 and move toward 1945. Rather, it unfolded from our own present-day moment; from "the now," the *Jetztzeit* (to use Walter Benjamin's term), placing our own present and future into the context of the promises, curses, and anxieties that we have inherited from history and that we exacerbate with contemporary practices. Every present is saturated with the past—or, rather, with multiple, layered pasts. We cannot get away from the past, nor do we often want to. We live on the surface—the wave (*die Welle*)—of history, memory, and culture. The Cassiers *Ring* strove to show how the globalized, late-capitalist moment of 2010 continues to build on the Wagnerian vocabularies—musical, linguistic, visual, political—of 1870. *Das Rheingold* offered (for Milan's benefit?) a surface style of mesmerizing and kaleidoscopic beauty, yielding slowly, deliberately, and inexorably to scenes of natural, human, and political degradation. Cassiers's is the *Ring* of the Anthropocene era.

The twenty-first century has accustomed us to multispatial living, with the cyberworld working perhaps as the most persuasive agent of such perception. Cassiers's stage design produced such multiple spatial worlds. In recognizing also the multitemporality of human experience, the condition of living in simultaneous, multiple time zones, it captured a way of living in history that is also fundamentally musical—indeed, a dimension of Wagner's music that had not previously been answered by a directorial or design correlative. Musically and dramatically, and by way of the toggle between action and narration, Wagner consistently asks us to live in multiple moments of his three-generation epic. The claims and experiments of photography, cubism, and other modernisms notwithstanding, our default visual instinct is to assume that an image occupies a single and consistent moment in time—perhaps especially so on a live theater stage. Our default perception holds on to G. E. Lessing's 1766 theorization of the difference between pictorial art forms and poetic and narrative ones as the difference between spatial proximity (what he called the principle of *Nebeneinander*) and linear temporality or sequence (*Nacheinander*).[9] Cassiers's stage, however, provided a visual match of multispatiality with multitemporality. Visually as well as musically, his audience faced multiple combinations of spatial and temporal planes.

Cassiers's stage realized this principle of space-time multiplicity through a strongly conceived and very beautiful aesthetic. This aesthetic works from the double entendre of "projection," as understood by Freud and others. On the one hand, projection is a photographic and cinematographic technology. An image is projected from a source onto a surface. A projection is also a psychic dynamic involving the externalization of inner experience and (in its symptomatic character) the displacement of the origins of emotions and symptoms onto a secondary, external source. Thus I can project onto you the responsibility for a problem that I have created—think of Wotan in *Das Rheingold* and beyond. The fact that a projection conventionally assumes and lands on a screen in fact made the "screen" a metaphorical prop for psychoanalysis. The screen is a physical pun: it both hides and reveals.

Based on this fundamental double meaning of "projection," Cassiers's

Ring can be understood to explore the nature of interactivity in ways that involve but are by no means limited to contemporary visual technologies. Wagner's *Ring* operates by projecting its massive material onto an audience. Wagner's own architectural design of the Bayreuth Festival Theater works as a literal acoustic realization of such projection. Recall that the famous covered orchestra pit throws its sound back toward the stage, where it blends with the voices, then is reprojected toward the audience. And the audience works (if we can assume an active, listening audience to be working) by experiencing, examining, and understanding both our reception of the work's projections—in sound and sight—alongside the simultaneous counterprojection from our own inner lives back onto and into the work. This inner life will contain, as part of its unlimited archive, the history of our responses to Wagner and the *Ring*. Such histories are at once individual and collective. Audience members will possess their own biographical and aesthetic "maps," which will place this important new traversal of the *Ring* in a historical emotional and aesthetic context. These contexts differ profoundly between the opera communities of Milan and Berlin.

The content of this dynamic of mutual projection will be varied. One key dimension will be the relation between the present moment and history and memory. History and memory and their relation to the fleeting present moment constitute a key theme of the *Ring* itself. As mentioned earlier, important recent Wagner scholarship has explored these issues by paying close attention to the relation between narration and action. Throughout the *Ring*, action is constantly interrupted and reinterpreted, even proactively, by narration. Wotan's monologue in act 2 of *Die Walküre* is the most massive of these interruptions but is by no means the only one. (Famously, when the musicologist Alfred Lorenz tried, in the 1930s, to explicate every opera and every act of the *Ring* as a manifestation of sonata form, the one event he could not integrate into the model was Wotan's monologue.) Think (among others) of Loge and Erda in *Das Rheingold*; Siegmund followed by Sieglinde in act 1 of *Die Walküre*; Mime in act 1 of *Siegfried*; the Norns in the *Götterdämmerung* prologue; and, finally, Siegfried's death scene in act 3 of *Götterdämmerung*. Indeed, the psychological depths of the characters grow as they begin to possess a strong sense of the past, which can both inform and impede action. (Indeed I believe I've already given away my own valuation, to wit, that Wagnerian narration as mature or late style is interrupted by action.)

Cassiers's conception and aesthetic point to a new way of understanding history in relation to the present moment. So it would appear that we are once again in the realm of history, but with a new historical epistemology. Here I return to the ideas of projection and interactivity. These two related technical and aesthetic practices in fact enable the double dialectic of past and present: one unfolding onstage, and one unfolding in the experience of the audience. In both cases we have a constantly shifting relationship between the past and the present, between, on the one hand, a past that is fixed and over but yet always variable in its reconstruction and, on the other, a present that is always vexed and tense in terms of the choices for action it presents and the outcomes for the future that it holds.

These two dialectics can be activated simultaneously by drawing the audience existentially into the actions and narrations unfolding onstage, as well into the memory of the past that transcends the story and temporality unfolding onstage, that is, the memory of past productions. In all cases, the past remains present in the form of traces and quotations, memories and returns.

When the action of *Das Rheingold* commences, we are simultaneously in 1850 and 2010. Fantasies of time travel invariably come down to this dual time consciousness. This duality speaks first to the way historical memory is experienced and historical knowledge is formed. Again Burckhardt: history is what one age finds of interest in another. But, even more than that, the same duality is in fact how time and history are actually experienced on the spectrum from, on one end, "living in the past" by way of nostalgic or traumatic repetition and reenactment to the products of analytic and interpretive distance, on the other. We live the "now," the current moment, on a continuum that incorporates memory and expectations. In Wagner's world and in Cassiers's, the three elements of past, present, and future remain evident—even at the very end of the *Ring*.

More specifically, *Das Rheingold* does bring us into the world of 1850, a moment defined, as Hannah Arendt has written, "by a rush for the most superfluous raw material on earth": gold. Gold, Arendt observed, is "the delusion of an absolute value."[10] As we know, the global economy operated on that principle until 1971, when the United States abandoned the gold standard. At the same time, however, Cassiers draws both Alberich and us, the audience, into the desire for gold through a dynamic that reflects contemporary forms of desire and, indeed, the artificial creation of desire. This is the world of visual stimulation, the world of advertising and the world of pornography. The two are points on a single spectrum. Gold is the first fictional absolute that drives the *Ring*. Gold signifies wealth and power. Desire for it breeds violence. Wotan and Alberich share this desire and share in its violence.

Scene 1 of Cassiers's *Rheingold* is set on a flat stage that meets a perpendicular upstage wall, a mosaic of dark-green and gold shimmering sparks that may signify the walls of the river. We are indeed underwater, and the stage floor is filled with a shallow pool, enough to create some playful or mocking splashing. The rear wall is also a screen. Onto the screen are projected images taken by two discreet cameras hanging down in full view of the audience. One by one, the Rhinemaidens peer and play into the cameras as if looking into a mirror, knowing also that their images will project onto the rear wall and serve further to seduce and taunt Alberich in his futile advances on them. The cunning and narcissism of these Rhinemaidens contradict any claim to the innocence of nature. Alberich, in turn, is fascinated by the cameras but clueless as to how to make them work in his favor. On us, the audience, the cameras also have some power. They implicate us in the scopophilia that Alberich is learning, bringing us even into a kind of pornophilia, as if we have come to the opera to reside, even momentarily, in a kind of chat room.

Wotan and Alberich meet in *Das Rheingold*'s third scene. In the design of Cassiers and his team, Alberich's Nibelheim headquarters has become a high-tech surveillance center (fig. 1.1). Alberich's pornographic curiosities of scene 1 (which also involve cameras) are now inflated into global scopophilia and media control. A mogul in a hypermediatized world, Alberich likes to watch but, like Fafner two operas later, doesn't know what to do with his scopic power. Toward the end of the evening, Wotan will differentiate himself from Alberich by also desiring knowledge and, possibly, love. These desires he will bequeath to his favorite children, Siegmund and Brünnhilde. Gold, love, and knowledge will continue to define the desires that drive the *Ring*.

3. *Les passions humaines*

Throughout the four scenes of this *Rheingold*, audiences gaze—whether they focus on it or not—upon a mysterious, multidimensional screen at the back of the stage. (Scenes 1 and 3 involve a partial double wall; scenes 2 and 4 offer a clear view of the back installation I introduce here.) Revealed sometimes in fragments and sometimes in its entirety, this screen is the recipient of multiple projections. Some of these projections offer shadows of

FIG. 1.1. *Das Rheingold*, scene 3: Alberich in Nibelheim. Photo: Koen Broos.

characters: the oversized shadows of the giants Fasolt and Fafner accompanying the human forms of the singers onstage; undersize representations of the goddess Freia as Fasolt and Fafner are subduing and then abducting her. Each of the giants has a double presence: the two singers appear more or less as themselves, in black suits, while the screen behind them contains their projected shadow images as giants (fig. 1.2). The image-giants are thus produced images of modern technology, while the human giants are the producers of their own images and projected power—not the hands of labor, but the forces in control of dark labor: countercapitalists, drone drivers.

When the screen itself claims attention, it emits in color and imagery an ecological correlative to the story. A seductive deep-blue eveningscape ac-

FIG. 1.2. *Das Rheingold*, scene 2: giants and landscape. Photo: Koen Broos.

companies the appearance of Erda and her grim seduction of Wotan. The Valhalla scene is supplied with a brilliant green hillscape, which on closer looks seems to present an entropic topography; the greenscape appears to degrade progressively into dying ridges, as if by strip mining. The degradation of landscape began, conceivably, with Wotan's construction of Valhalla and correlates, as the plot develops, with the intensification of his moral compromises. The morphing of Romantic landscape into images of vast waste recalls, in style and scale, the images of the photographer Edward Burtynsky.

The rear screen itself is built of thick slabs of translucent fiberglass, deeply textured to produce the effect of a bas-relief. And this turns out to be the case. At the opera's end, the material surface of the screen itself is clearly identified, basking in a glorious but also slightly sickening hue of gold. Now functioning as the gateway to Valhalla, the huge golden screen provides a cynical riff on Lorenzo Ghiberti's doors of the Florence baptistry. As the screen lifts to allow the gods to pass under it, the riff on the gates of paradise reinforces Wotan's delusion and the audience's unease, confronted

FIG. 1.3. *Das Rheingold*, scene 2: gods. Photo: Michael P. Steinberg.

now with the image content of the bas-relief (fig. 1.3). Now the screen reveals its source: it is a recreation of Jef Lambeaux's 1898 bas-relief *Les passions humaines*.

At the close of *Das Rheingold* and the transition from the *Ring*'s prologue into the actual drama, the emergence into view of the Lambeaux frieze supplies the visual leitmotif that will anchor and define the stage from this moment on. Standing between Wagner's moment and our own, this fin-de-siècle monument to human excess offers a kind of profane riff on Michelangelo's *Last Judgment*.

In 1889, on the recommendation of Alphonse Balat, favorite architect of King Leopold II of Belgium, the young Victor Horta was commissioned for 100,000 francs to design a pavilion for an important spot at the corner of the Cinquantenaire Park in Brussels, a space planned and named for the fiftieth anniversary commemoration of Belgian independence in 1880. The following year King Leopold commissioned the Antwerp-born sculptor Jef Lambeaux to fill the pavilion with a sculptural frieze, of which the result was *Les passions humaines*. Horta's structure is an early example of the art nouveau, or *Jugendstil*, style which he would help define: its correct neoclassicism is subverted by strong elements of subversive organicism. At first glance the building looks like a classic temple. However, there is not a single straight line in the building. Slightly bent like the foot of a tree, the walls seem to have sprung up organically from the foundation.

The pavilion has a turbulent history. Originally intended for the 1897 Brussels International Exposition and completed in time, its opening was delayed until 1899 because of a conflict between architect and artist. On the day of the inauguration, 1 October 1899, the unfinished temple stood open, with the relief visible from the surrounding park. Forced to close off the temple with a wooden barricade, Horta left it unfinished until, shortly after Lambeaux's death in 1908, he acceded to Lambeaux's wishes by building a wall that would permanently hide the bas-relief with a closed front to enhance the natural light coming through the glass roof.

In 1967, on the occasion of a state visit to Belgium by King Faisal ibn Abdal-Aziz of Saudi Arabia, King Baudouin I gave the pavilion in a ninety-nine-year leasehold as a gift to the Saudi king for use as a museum of Islamic art, together with the East Pavilion of the 1880 National Exhibition, which would later become the Great Mosque of Brussels. The building belongs legally to the nonprofit Islamic Cultural Centre of Belgium, of which the ambassador of Saudi Arabia to Belgium is the chairman. The pavilion and the Lambeaux relief were protected by a royal decree on 18 November 1976. Two years later, the donation to King Khalid of Saudi Arabia was made official by the royal decree of 12 September 1979. Until 2015 and the completion of a material restoration, the pavilion remained mostly closed to the public and the Lambeaux frieze doubly hidden behind a protective curtain. The frieze is disturbing. How and whom it disturbs, however, is an interesting question, and one not irrelevant to its second life on a Wagnerian stage.

Lambeaux had presented a draft on paper of his relief *Les passions humaines* to the Triennial Salon of Ghent in 1889. It generated immediate controversy. A conceivably neomannerist and secular reply to *The Last Judgment*, the work depicts human bodies entangled in poses suggestive of erotic bliss and physical torture, intimacy and violence, eros and thanatos, love and death. It also suggests scenes of war, rape, and suicide. A winged figure, possibly an angel of death, hovers at top center. The upper left quadrant highlights an orgiastic grouping in agitated motion above two tiny caverns, one filled with a mother and child, the other with an adult male-female couple. On the right are supine and contorted male bodies in scenes of war and body-to-body combat, overseen by a male body attached by shackles to a horizontal beam over his head. This figure has been seen as a crucifixion, though the visual reference is unclear.

The journal *L'art moderne* in 1890 described the work as "a pile of naked and contorted bodies, muscled wrestlers in delirium, an absolute and incomparable childish concept. It is at once chaotic and vague, bloated and pretentious, pompous and empty.... And what if, instead of paying 300,000 francs for the 'passions,' the government simply bought works of art?" The possible off-center representation of or reference to the Crucifixion caused particular controversy among Catholic viewers. More recently, the work in general was considered incompatible with the Saudi leasehold.

Like Cassiers and his Toneelhuis-based team, Jef Lambeaux is closely identified with the city of Antwerp. He was born there in 1852, and in 1887 the city revealed his best-known work, which has since remained as ostentatiously visible as *Les passions humaines* has remained hidden. Anchoring the city's Grand Place, or Grote Markt, in front of the city hall (completed in 1889) is the massive sculptural depiction of Silvius Brabo, the Roman captain who, according to local legend, founded the city after slaying a giant, cutting off the giant's enormous hand and throwing it into the sea. The name Antwerp derives from the Dutch words *hand werpen*—the throwing of the hand.

The Belgian fin de siècle produced massive urban renewal and architectural performance in Brussels, Antwerp, and other cities in a material correlative of King Leopold II's drive to transform the country into an empire. At home, Belgian cityscapes competed with Second Empire Paris and its mid-century reorganization under the authority of Napoleon III and Baron Haussmann. The Belgian project was financed by the colonial control of the African Congo region and its material resources, especially rubber. The Belgian constitutional monarchy offered limited power to its sovereign, but in 1885 the Belgian parliament authorized Leopold to rule over a large swath of Africa, control its native population, and mine its resources as a personal enterprise. The naming of the "Congo Free State" followed and endured until 1908. This story of imperial brutalization has been told by Adam Hochschild in his widely read book *King Leopold's Ghost*.[11] Recently Debora Silverman has connected the reality and imaginary of the Belgian Congo and its rubber vines to some of the leading visual motifs of art nouveau, in particular the vinelike forms of Victor Horta. As Silverman writes:

By 1905, two decades of contact with the Congo Free State had remade Belgium into a global hub, vitalized by a tentacular economy and technological prowess. Steamer ships loaded to bursting disgorged previous cargoes at Antwerp harbor, from ivory tooth tusks and exotic fruits to colossal and colored hardwoods. Most unusual were the cakes, disks, and coils of latex extracted from reportedly infinite supplies of wild rubber vines draping the Conga forests, described by gleeful contemporaries as a providential windfall that fell "like manna from heaven" into the laps of lucky Belgians and their generous and audacious king.[12]

Similarly, Silverman observes that, for his Antwerp statue of Brabo, "Lambeaux reached back to the legends of the city's origins to create a symbol of the new vitality of Antwerp in the imperial age, casting a colossal statue not of a messenger of the gods but of a soldier of vengeance."[13]

As the nineteenth century closed, Lambeaux's Brabo statue took on a grisly new referentiality. Between 1897 and 1905, as both Hochschild and Silverman have recounted, British and other merchants and agents returning to the ports of Antwerp and Liverpool from Africa revealed the Belgian colonial practice of severing the hands of Congo natives. Amputation of the hand was perhaps the most flagrant of the Belgians' violent practices, which also included slave labor, public torture, and the wholesale burning of villages. In Silverman's account, it was "the product of a vicious accounting system which required that native troops, whose ammunition was carefully rationed, present Belgian post commanders with a severed hand for every villager killed as proof that they had not wasted bullets."[14] The severed hand thus became, in Silverman's eloquent summary, "the visual unconscious of Belgian colonialism."[15]

The general political unconscious of Cassiers's production stretches back from the Burtynskylike images of environmental degradation to the period of the 1870s—the decade of the unveiling of the *Ring* and of German (and other) imperial designs in Europe and abroad. Europe's eyes were on Africa as the next alleged *terra nullius* available for colonial invasion. In 1884-85 the German imperial government hosted the Berlin Conference, also known as the Congo Conference, which achieved the division and regulation of European colonialism in Africa. The inscription into the production of the Belgian-African visual unconscious, including but also beyond the images of Lambeaux's *Passions humaines*, will come into relief with *Götterdämmerung*.

PLATE 1. *Das Rheingold*, scene 1: Alberich's scopophilia; Rhinemaidens' hands. Photo: Koen Broos.

PLATE 2. *Das Rheingold*, scene 2: giants and landscape. Photo: Koen Broos.

PLATE 3. *Das Rheingold*, scene 4: gods. Photo: Michael P. Steinberg.

PLATE 4. *Die Walküre*, act 1: Hunding's hut. Photo: Koen Broos.

PLATE 5. *Götterdämmerung*, prologue: Norns. Photo: Koen Broos.

PLATE 6. *Götterdämmerung*, act 1: Brünnhilde's rock and fire. Photo: Koen Broos.

PLATE 7. *Götterdämmerung*, act 3: Siegfried's death. Photo: Koen Broos.

PLATE 8. *Götterdämmerung*, act 3: Brünnhilde's immolation. Photo: Koen Broos.

4. *W* and *G*

If *Das Rheingold* (which is about building blocks) discloses some of the building blocks of Wagner's sonic universe, it also discloses the habits and pretensions of his phonic one. Recall that, for better or worse, Wagner's words carry sonic—possibly musical—values, positive and negative. Heavily consonant driven (not surprisingly for German), his words and their sounds cathect to the vocalized consonants. The *w* and the *l* are the most preferred among his—and his characters'—consonant sounds, the (hard) *g* the most reviled. Characters loved and cared for by the musical-dramatic texture in which they appear—Siegmund, for example—emphasize the "good" consonants in their speech/song. Characters with ambiguous moral or aesthetic dignity—Wotan, certainly, but also Alberich—toggle between consonant worlds.

Conceivably, the letter *w* carried the announcement of Wagner's own name, becoming a kind of performative invocation of him. If we recall Nietzsche's speculation about Wagner's anxiety that the actor Ludwig Geyer might have been his biological father, then the opposition of the good *w* and the bad *g* has an additional sonic and ideological aura. Alberich's ugliness, and especially his much-commented-upon sonic ugliness, highlights the hard *g*: *gartig glättrich glittriche Glimmer*, and so on. Introducing the gods at the start of scene 2, Wagner gives them the clear benefit of any moral or aesthetic doubt. The Valhalla universe fits into a harmonic musical grammar and texture, starting with the exposition of the so-called Valhalla leitmotif, which announces the scene. The *embourgeoisement* of the godly couple Wotan and Fricka emerges via a standard marital spat about male mobility. Here again, Wotan receives the Wagnerian sonic and ideological nod through the emphasis of the *w*:

> Wandel und Wechsel liebt wer lebt ...

> To live is to love change and exchange ...

Through a kind of inherited sonic unconscious, Siegmund, in act 1 of *Die Walküre*, will echo his lost father's locutionary elegance through the same practice of the repeated *w* followed by the repeated *l*:

> Winterstürme wichen
> dem Wonnemond,—

> in mildem Lichte
> leuchtet der Lenz;—
> auf linden Lüften
> leicht und lieblich,
> Wunder webend
> er sich wiegt;
>
> Wintry storms give way to the pull of the moon;
> in a gentle light
> springtime shines forth
> On balmy breezes
> light and lovely
> it weaves
> miracles as it wafts.

Now, these same consonant sounds and ideologies can become ironized when uttered by different kinds of characters, either knowingly or not. Loge, for example, seems actually aware of these mechanisms in a way that—here as elsewhere—cannily exceeds the self-awareness of Wotan. He begins his extraordinary monologue in scene 2 of *Das Rheingold* with the lament

> Immer ist Undank Loges Lohn.
>
> Ingratitude is always Loge's reward.

Through the repeated *l*'s of the phrase "Loges Lohn," Loge signals to Wotan, "I know your game, including your sonic one."

Loge's position is that of essential advisor to Wotan and the gods; he is not one of them and does not follow them into Valhalla. He is Bleichröder to Wotan's Bismarck, Kissinger to Wotan's Nixon. Patrice Chéreau was entirely justified, in 1976, in shaping him (with the help of Heinz Zednik's labile performance) into a figure reminiscent of Moses Mendelssohn: hunchbacked, bespectacled, ironic, but taken with perfect seriousness by the mainstream elite. Inevitably here, but with great subtlety, Loge/Zednik's articulation of the words and sounds "Loges Lohn" embodied a basic anti-Semitic anxiety, whereby the Jew can approximate the German by imitating his language.

Cassiers's interest did not pursue this direction at all. At the same time, a unique vocabulary—in this case a visual one—invoked the suggestion of Loge as gifted imitator. Cassiers hired the choreographer Sidi Larbi Cherkaoui to develop and insert a dance dimension into the evening. A dozen dancers embodied the demiurges of nature during the three orchestral transitions between scenes (these visual dimensions were initially greeted by the audience with some irritation). A more precise function and meaning of the dance and dancers involved the embodiment of auras for the gods, so that the gods—including Loge—shared their emotions and gestures with a dancing double. These dancing auras occasionally affirmed the expressed emotions of the characters, doubling in body language what the singer/character stated in text, music, and gesture. Just as often, the aura contradicted the stated utterance, implying the presence of a kind of body unconscious—an inner ambivalence or contradiction (*Zwiespalt*). Cassiers's compatriot Maurice Béjart had developed a similar notion for a *Don Giovanni* that I saw in Geneva in 1980. Cassiers's dancing auras were more precise. Only the gods had them, and they disappeared from the story at the end of *Das Rheingold*, amounting retrospectively to a privilege or prop of the gods that faded out as their old-regime legitimacy degraded. (As rehearsals progressed for the La Scala premiere, the dance elements were reduced, often as a result of the persuasive interventions of the general director, Stéphane Lissner, who attended most rehearsals. Erda's entrance on a hydraulic lift, for example, was originally accompanied by a kind of magnetic draw of the dancers toward her and away from the other gods. But this addition seemed to many of us a distraction from this internally fully auratic moment rather than an enhancement of it, and the dance element was omitted.)

For the most part, the singer gods treated their dancer doubles as benign nuisances. No problem here, as this attitude correlates with Wotan and his family's likely dismissal of their own unconscious. Only on one occasion did one of the singers attempt to duplicate movements of his/her dancing aura: Loge, at the start of his monologue, just after the lament "Immer ist Undank Loges Lohn" and during the orchestral mini-interlude that introduces his story—between, *pace* music drama, recitative and aria—added his own physical pirouette to those of both the orchestra and his dancing double. Stefan Rügamer performed the role, and this sudden supplement to his extraordinary vocal and linguistic articulation and lyricism became one of the full production's most unexpected and magical moments. Loge is about to instruct Wotan in the art of cynical power politics—*Machtpolitik*—recounting Alberich's theft of the gold on the basis of the renunciation of love and ultimately recommending that Wotan simply rob Alberich of the gold and the new products and emblems of powers that Alberich and his slaves have fashioned from it: the Ring and the Tarnhelm. Loge's (and soon Wotan's) Machiavellian moment begins with a musical nostalgia for innocence, an element that Rügamer was able to double through his own brief dance movement and its reinvocation of a world before language.

Perhaps the most successful deployment of the dancing auras involved their collective embodiment of the Tarnhelm, the helmet that Alberich fashions from the Rhinegold that enables its bearer to assume any manner of disguise. In scene 3 of *Das Rheingold*, which involves Alberich's hubris and his entrapment by Loge and Wotan, the dancers intertwined to form a kind of human throne that coddled Alberich and menaced his uninvited visitors with snapping, tentacular arms. (In scene 4, when Alberich is forced to surrender his power and equipment to Wotan, the Tarnhelm entrapped and restrained him; at this point it answered only to Wotan and Loge.)

Now, in scene 3, Loge inhabits his alliance with Wotan, perhaps unaware that his social position is just as close, if not closer, to Alberich's. In his momentary hubris and swagger, Alberich imitates Wotan, and not unsuccessfully at that, if the orchestral support undergirding the moment is to be taken seriously. Accusing the gods of reveling in condescension to the *Schwarzalbe* (black dwarf) of Nibelheim, Alberich sings:

> Auf wonnigen Höh'n,
> in seligem Weben
> wiegt ihr euch;
> den Schwarzalben
> verachtet ihr ewigen Schwelger! —
>
> On radiant heights
> You pamper and coddle yourselves
> Despising the black dwarf
> In your endless hedonism.

Alberich appears to have momentarily gained control of the orchestra and thereby of the *Ring* epic itself. The orchestra itself now displays its capacity to modulate from a producer of sonic nobility into a kind of sadistic machine. Alberich's Wotanisms become all the more successful when they are fully vocalized and sung by a strong bass-baritone rather than snarled by a character singer. The vocal and ideological stakes of Alberich and Wotan resemble those of Beckmesser. The highstakes duality or difference between Alberich and Wotan, both of whom steal the ring through the course of *Das Rheingold*, juxtaposes a crime of rage and instinct against one of entitlement and structure. In Slavoj Žižek's recent summary: "With reference to Brecht's famous 'What is the robbery of a bank compared to the founding of a new bank?,' one is tempted to say: 'What is a poor Jew's stealing of the gold compared to the violence of the Aryan's [Wotan's] grounding of the rule of Law?'"[16]

Alberich's initial introduction of the Tarnhelm (to his indentured brother Mime and to us) is accompanied both by the Tarnhelm chords—a kind of musical rhyme in minor mode—and by a kind of hocus-pocus conjuring with a typical consonant *Stabreim*:

> Nacht und Nebel,
> Niemand gleich ...
>
> Night and fog
> Resembling no one ...

The language has a considerable aura for audiences today. The moniker "Nacht und Nebel" was attached—with a deliberate reference to *Das Rheingold*—to a directive that Adolf Hitler issued in December 1941 authorizing the "disappearance" of suspected resistance figures. All information about the victims' fates vanished as well. This aura accompanies the resonances of the word *gleich* as well, which, in addition to its principal meaning here of "resembling," also means "momentarily," as if to signify that "in a moment there will be no one." Alberich may control this second meaning himself, as he deploys the Tarnhelm to effect his own momentary disappearance.[17] The term *vernebelt* (reduced to mist) subsequently entered Nazi usage. In 1955 Alain Resnais used the phrase (translated as *Nuit et brouillard*) as the title of his documentary about Auschwitz. The Tarnhelm is not incidental to these usages, for it has itself become a metaphor for the modulations, disguises, and wanderings of sounds, words, meaning, and reference.

TWO

Siegmund's Death

1. Eros and Civilization

RICHARD WAGNER CALLED *DIE WALKÜRE* THE "FIRST EVENING" of *Der Ring des Nibelungen*; he called *Das Rheingold* the prologue or *Vorabend*. Musically and dramatically, we are introduced to a radically new and different world when the opening bars of *Die Walküre* resound. A fully developed orchestral palette of leitmotifs paints a wild storm scene, and the curtain rises on a modest dwelling: a fully human scene that has nothing to do with the gods, dwarves, and nymphs of *Das Rheingold*. At the same time, however, the way *Die Walküre* portrays radical beginnings reveals some telling reminiscences of the unfolding of *Das Rheingold*.

Das Rheingold began with a musical allegory of the birth of the universe. The human story of *Die Walküre* opens with a musical and dramatic portrayal of the origins of human contact, communication, sentiment, intimacy, and eros. The encounter of Siegmund and Sieglinde begins on a level prior to all forms of communicative expression. Their music then intensifies gradually, as if musical forms were at once producing and reflecting the power of personal interaction. When the discovery of love reaches its expressive correlative, the music is not only capable of participating in the experience of love but essential to it.

Guy Cassiers and Enrico Bagnoli's scenic design for act 1 of *Die Walküre* participates in the unfolding of the drama. The core set is a simple concave screen, a geometric abstraction that represents Hunding's hut in terms of both space and scale. The remaining stage space, the extensions of Hunding's walls and the stage screen that represents them, resemble tree bark: the architecture of nature that both menaces, as in the opening storm, and protects (fig. 2.1). The space is at once orienting and disorienting, protective and threatening. Boundaries between inside and outside space are unstable, as are the boundaries of protected and unprotected space. Interior space (home and hearth) is not readily distinguishable from outside space; the home may not protect from the raging storm. Home spaces and family

FIG. 2.1. *Die Walküre*, act 1: Hunding's hut. Photo: Koen Broos.

structures are in this respect the locations of the uncanny: the *unheimlich* (literally, the unhomely), where the familiar and the alienating converge.

The screen provides acoustic benefits to the singers, for it catches their sound and sends it back to the audience. As a receiver of projections, the screen also mediates between the exterior and interior of the hut. The ambiguity of literal spatial interiors and exteriors has an analog in the play of the inner thoughts and outward expressions of the characters. The interior of the hut is unmarked except for the tree that grips the sword that Wotan, having appeared portentously at Sieglinde's wedding, lodged there in the hope that Siegmund would claim both it and Sieglinde herself. The water that consoles Siegmund in the first scene is also there. Everything else remains abstract, including the table that Sieglinde sets for her hostile husband and their mysterious guest.

The instability and uncanniness of "home" also marks and complicates the rules of hospitality. We are reminded that the etymology of "host," closely related to "guest" and—more obviously—to "hospitality" and its variants, also links the word to "hostile." Hunding obeys an apparent synthesis of hospitality and hostility, inviting Siegmund to spend the night but to fight in the morning. (Chéreau's Hunding arrived in the company of a bunch of henchmen, a menacing and convincing variation that Chéreau attributed to Hollywood westerns.)

Perhaps Hunding need not be evil incarnate to express immediate hostility at the encounter of an unknown man at home with his wife. His attitude receives confirmation when Siegmund reveals that their day's activities involved fighting on opposing sides of a traumatic family dispute. Prior to that legitimation, Hunding notes the resemblance of his wife and her guest: the look in their eye has a strange affinity, an observation that Wagner has Hunding note as "der gleissende Wurm glänzt auch ihm aus dem Auge" (the glistening worm [or dragon] gleams from his eye too). This odd image of a worm or dragon is potentially ratified by casting possibilities, since the bass who sings Hunding can be efficiently and convincingly cast as the two Fafners: the human giant in *Rheingold* and the dragon in *Siegfried*. The dragon Fafner, as we'll see in the following chapter, comes to connote the depths in which the unconscious lives. The man Fafner (for whom Wagner wrote too little in *Rheingold*) and the character Hunding share the bass voice—and possibly the same singer's bass voice—with the dragon Fafner, adding a sonic depth to the *Ring*'s vocal palette that echoes the orchestra's deep brass and low strings. Hunding's voice thus has a depth and violence that are more interesting and more menacing than Hunding the character. More important here is the suggestion that music drama knows more than Hunding: through its deep sonorities and its sometimes odd tropes—including the worm/dragon in all its formations—it shows a capacity to engage the unconscious. The worm in the eye of Siegmund and Sieglinde marks the power of the unconscious; Hunding is seeing something here, though he is incapable of understanding it.

Scene 2, marked "Siegmund alone" in Wagner's stage directions, moves Siegmund into a music of epiphany. In plot and leitmotivic terms, his narrative recalls his father's promise of a magic sword that would deliver him from danger. The sword, we know, is there, and the music doesn't hesitate to remind us. But beneath the trumpet's play of the sword motif lodge the discovery, formation, and articulation of desire. Let's acknowledge the obvious by following the combination of desire and sword into the discovery of the phallus. But let's also avoid the meeting of cliché and cleverness to leave ample room for the stunning arc of the second and third scenes of this act, which open a world of pure desire and innocence that the social, political, and legal systems of act 2 will make every effort to destroy. Whereas Tristan will assume that pure desire cannot mix with social reality and must remain restricted to the realm of the night, Siegmund in his exultant naiveté will unleash desire (his and Sieglinde's) by the light of the moon and then attempt to rush out with her into the open world.

When, according to Wagner's stage directions, the moon bursts onto the scene, the screen opens to reveal the forest beyond: trees in the form of thin white plastic columns. Abstraction reigns here too. But the bare ciphers of trees lining Cassiers and Bagnoli's upstage invite questions and observations that will gain momentum in the thicker forest of act 2. Projections on the trees will approximate letters and numbers, reminiscent perhaps of some of the tubular installations of Jenny Holzer (fig. 2.2). But they remain illegible, reminding us of the illegibility of nature.

The mystery of the forest also cradles unfathomable violence, culminating in the murder of Siegmund by Hunding, in unexpected (and short-lived) alliance with Wotan. The illegibility of the forest is displayed visually here, and in act 2 of *Siegfried* Wagner will make the point acoustically through the sounds of the Forest Bird. In a kind of magical moment, however, Siegfried will understand the words of the suddenly anthropomorphized Forest Bird, thereby closing the human-animal and human-forest gap and their illegibilities. This step opens the question addressed in the introduction with respect to *Lohengrin*: is this knowledge in fact psychotic, therefore potentially fatal, and a sign of Siegfried's doom?

Act 2 of *Die Walküre* brings together the godly world (Wotan, Fricka, and Brünnhilde) and the human one (Siegmund, Sieglinde, and Hunding) with ferocity. In human and historical terms, the confrontation is between high

FIG. 2.2. *Die Walküre*, act 2: Inscrutable forest. Photo: Koen Broos.

and low society, between power and poverty, between the well-connected and the isolated. These gods sustain their authority through never-ending warfare. Cassiers and Bagnoli thus accompany the thunderous act 2 prelude with suggestions of the iconography of mediatized warfare: their flashing green lights recall the censored visual transmission of "embedded" cameras in the Gulf War of 1990. The horses of Wotan, Fricka, and all the Valkyries—both imposing and mangled—are shown in act 2 and act 3 as both instruments and victims of violence and war.

"There is no document of culture that is not at the same time a document of barbarism." Walter Benjamin wrote this now canonic sentence at the start of the Second World War, which he would not survive. His comment engages not only history itself but also the understanding of history in scholarship and the arts. It may fit no document of culture better than the work of Wagner and its double status as a profound analysis of the convergence of culture and barbarism as well as a symptom of the same. At the center of the *Ring* and its peripeteia in act 2 of *Die Walküre* lies the tetralogy's core and central problem, which is also the central problem of Wagner's career and legacy: the interrelation of culture and barbarism, beauty and violence, violence and knowledge. This is Wotan's story, and it is also Wagner's. Wotan does retain his will to know the world, indeed to know beyond the world that he is able to create and control. His entrapment overcomes his will to knowledge and any redemptive capacity it may retain. Music drama enters a similar ambiguity as both a discourse of exploration and human insight on the one hand and a system—perhaps a closed one—on the other. Listening intently to its combined texture and pulse, we are able to open its warp and weft to reveal an analytical, self-analytical, and deconstructive capacity on the part of both the work and, potentially, its composer. Opening this possibility involves listening against both the work's and the composer's devotees (including the leitmotif cartographers) and its best critics (Adorno above all).

Wotan's story began with his unsuccessful theft of the gold and the ring from Alberich, who had himself stolen it from the Rhine. Wotan's bungled transaction succeeded only in transferring the gold, the ring, and their power from a Nibelung to a sleeping giant, in other words from an agent of active ignorance to one of passive ignorance. There was little doubt, as Wotan entered Valhalla, that he would strive to regain his booty, and that he would seek out Erda in order to do so. Wotan's interest in Erda was both strategic and erotic, and so was ours, the audience's. Wotan's strategy: the creation of a family as a mediator between the personal world and the public world, in other words between eros and love on the one side, wealth and power on the other. To an extent, we can say that this kind of politics exists at the foundation of mythology and tragedy, from the Norse and Icelandic sources of Wagner's gods to the ancient Greek cosmology at the source of Homer and Sophocles. Sophocles' corrupt King Creon, for example, complicit in the deaths of his brother Oedipus's children, is unable to choose between love, duty, and reasons of state. Sophocles' tragedy *Antigone* became a central reference in the nineteenth-century Germans' love of drama and its philosophical power. Wotan, however, neither has nor serves a state. He struggles between the private world and universe. Yet for him just as for Creon, the family becomes not only the mediator between private and public, but the instrument of that mediation. For these reasons, Shaw was right to place the plot of the *Ring* in the context of capitalism and the "laws" of unbridled enterprise, rather than within the politics of states and nations. Meet Wotan, Inc., a multinational corporation.

But Wotan, Inc., wants to stack his corporate board with family members, hence the plot of *Die Walküre*. It is here that Wotan's modernity is revealed, as his power is compromised by forced adherence to contracts: "Der Verträge bin ich nun Knecht" (I am enslaved by contracts), he confesses to Brünnhilde. He has replaced one binding transaction—the promise of Freia to the giants as payment for the building of Valhalla—with another, the ceding of the gold and ring. In order both to honor and to escape the contract, Wotan has arranged for his twin children, Siegmund and Sieglinde, to find each other and beget Siegfried, whose removal from Wotan by two generations will provide the legal technicality that will enable him to recover the gold and ring for Wotan under cover of his own alleged free agency. But Wotan's sidestepping of the law of inheritance does not protect him from the laws of marriage. Presumably, his chief legal advisor, Loge, a bachelor, did not take this into account. Wotan's consort, Fricka, whose portfolio includes the laws of marriage and thus the maintenance of the taboos on infidelity and incest, ruins the plan. Wotan's coerced obedience to these legal strictures thus forces him to turn his violence on his own children, resulting in the murder of his son Siegmund and the abuse and ruin of his daughter Brünnhilde. Indeed, in an early presentation of the concept of the Cassiers production to the administration of the Berlin State Opera, its general director, Jürgen Flimm, underscored the brutality of *Die Walküre*'s conclusion. The majestic melancholy of Wotan's farewell, Flimm cautioned, should not camouflage the baseness and vileness of his plan to cast her into the street to be raped—"fucked" was the word Flimm used—by any random passer-by.

2. Incest as a Cultural Code

For the nineteenth century, the multigenerational family emerges as at once the meeting point and the breaking point between the traditional world of community, honor, and affect and the contemporary world of society, exchange, and commodification. When the family turns inward, it experiences and represents itself according to bonds of affect—perhaps even love. When it turns outward to the world, or indeed when it conducts its own internal relations according to its internalization of external worldly rules, it becomes an organ of power. According to this economy, love and interiority are feminized; power and self-assertion are masculinized. Generational continuity is defined patriarchally: a continuation of name, capital, property, and power. The continuity of love is much more difficult to trace rationally, because love depends on the subjective energy created by specific personal relations.

In the nineteenth-century bourgeois family, bonds of love appear in configurations and tropes that go against the grain of the generational transmission of power and capital. A principal site of this kind of relationship is that between brother and sister. In nineteenth-century literature, the brother-sister relation is indeed a classic site of the countermodernizing affective bond. Sibling relations don't fit into the rationalization of the family as a political economy of productivity—of the creation of dynasties and capital. In this new world, the affective bonds between siblings easily collapses into violence as one brother claims the mantle of capital formation: Fafner against Fasolt, Alberich against Mime, even Siegfried against his phony brother Gunther. The relationship between brother and sister comes to be understood as a place of true impasse between affective and rationalized relations.

The intensity of the brother-sister relationship in this period and its erotic charge often leads to the classification of incest. David Warren Sabean has suggested that

> the relationship between brothers and sisters was an absolutely central theme for the post-Napoleonic German family. Heinz Reif in his study of the Paderborn nobility demonstrates that the new bourgeois family ideals during this period became characteristic even of the provincial nobility: Domesticity (*Innerlichkeit*), friendship, marriage and courtship based on emotion and individualization and sentimental cohesiveness were valued. Familial relations came to be marked by intense inner experience and the construction of personal connections based on feeling, with a tendency to develop individualized ways of expression. In this period appears among families from the nobility to the *Bildungsbürgertum* a new emphasis on dyadic relationships, which partly at least excluded others in the family. There was a great interest in letter writing to address individuals in the family and to construct special relations among those of the same age. Above all, this was a time for brothers and sisters to construct individual emotional relationships.[1]

In 1800, Sabean writes, the Wittenberg theologian Carl Nitzsch contrasted the purity of brother-sister love with the impurity and selfishness of marital love, in which lust is associated with egotism. Paradoxically, the designation of brother-sister love as the purest love functions as an eroticizing agent. German literature between 1770 and 1830 was saturated with stories of conscious and unconscious incest. The actual relationship between Johann Wolfgang von Goethe and his sister Cornelia has been dubbed incestuous by psychoanalytic observers and has been called the "very nerve center of Goethe's creativity" by one of them: Kurt Eissler. Only slightly less renowned—and no less significant—are the cases of Felix and Fanny Mendelssohn and Heinrich and Ulrike von Kleist. In all these cases, sympathy and attraction were nurtured by a sense of equality in education and temperament in childhood. The male sibling, however, as Sabean points out, reserved the mantle of public life for himself.

Erotic affectivity between brother and sister is further coded as a specifically early nineteenth-century phenomenon in another way. That is its incorporation of the Romantic notion of androgyny. In the musings of the Schlegel brothers' Athenäum circle, androgyny was prized as the harmonization of male and female personae that is the richest fount of creativity. For bourgeois brothers and sisters slotted into a socially and patriarchally sanctioned protocol of aesthetic education, the recognition of a counter-gendered version of the self in the sibling provided a flirtation with androgyny. The twin becomes the literary ideal type for this potential: the face that is the cross-gendered replication of the self. Thus, in Wagner's Siegmund and Sieglinde, we have a late—not a first—instance of this ideal type. For the male sibling—for Goethe and Felix Mendelssohn, for example—the culturally sanctioned course of this aesthetic education and its flirtation with androgyny was the final resumption of a secure masculinity—a separation from the sister that involved precisely the insistence that she restrict her talents to the home while he takes his out into the world.

The incestuous union of Siegmund and Sieglinde that lies at the center of the *Ring*'s plot thus also places the *Ring* at the center of nineteenth-century familial and social networks. Siegmund, in his unique psychological delicacy and complexity, embodies the complexity and vulnerability of a transitional generation from family business to systemic capitalism. His life traces mid-century Germany's cultural and political transition from liberal hope to violent betrayal. His personality marks the hope and defeat of a subjectivity combining inner life and ethical action. His music marks the same moment, the same hope and defeat.

The idea of Siegmund—Wotan's idea—is signaled by the sudden appearance of the so-called sword motif at the conclusion of *Das Rheingold*. The character Siegmund appears at the opening of *Die Walküre*. Were we to imagine the shape of the *Ring* as a concerto, then Siegmund enters the work in the position of the solo instrument. Here he resembles in the Countess in *The Marriage of Figaro*. But whereas Siegmund's entrance, like the Countess's, comes at the opening of the second part of a four-part structure, it carries additional privilege as the opening gesture in the first of three music dramas, as preceded by a prologue—the status Wagner accords explicitly to *Das Rheingold*.

In this first act of *Die Walküre*, Siegmund is granted exceptional privilege in the tuning of his own first-person voice—of his combination of self-awareness and self-presentation. He is given permission, one might say, by music drama to construct carefully his own musical and psychological subjectivity. This "permission" can be understood as a gesture of temporary hospitality on the part of music drama, a parallel to the momentary hospitality granted by his hostile host, Hunding. Siegmund is both at the center of music drama and its guest. He finds his voice, through the course of the first act, through two sudden and conflicting engagements: one with an erotic counterpart and one with his paternal inheritance.

In his narrative to Sieglinde and Hunding, Siegmund recalls his wandering childhood with his father, whom he refers to as Wälse. Wälse and his son were pariahs of the social world. They intervened to impose justice. They had different values. They were, as Hunding states in growing agitation, "ein wildes Geschlecht" (a wild breed), hated by all.

Siegmund's nobility, to Wagner's eye and ear, seems clear enough. What is less clear is the nature of Wagner's identification with Siegmund. An initial element is a projection of the thwarted revolutionary: Siegmund and Richard as impeded heroes of the 1848 revolts and their agendas. More mysteriously, Wagner's identification with Siegmund conjures the trope of the social pariah in its various symbolic manifestations. Wälse the Flying Dutchman, alias Ahasuerus, the Wandering Jew, has a son, whom he loves, trains, abandons, and finally kills. The structure of Richard's own fantasmatic relation of issues of paternity and filiation with respect to this cluster is rich. Wagner's own biography involves anxiety about his biological paternity and about his abandonment, through death, by his father. It involves his anxiety about his father's possibly having been his stepfather, his mother's second husband, the actor Ludwig Geyer, of whom he was fond. Geyer was, technically, a mime. From mime to Mime—to the allegory of the false, Jewish father—the distance is short. Wagner suspected that Geyer was his father and that Geyer was Jewish, which he was not. There is the vexed musical filiation of two prominent composers of Wagner's youth, Meyerbeer and Mendelssohn, whom Wagner disowned in the wake of his sense of having been abandoned by them. Finally, there is Wagner the megalomaniac, identifying with Christ himself, the original and absolute Son abandoned by his Jewish father: the "old God," to use Nietzsche's label for Wotan. Wagner-Siegmund-Christ: the son trained, loved, and killed by the Jewish father in the name of justice. (Not coincidentally, during the years of the initial sketches for the *Ring*, Wagner also worked on a spoken drama called *Jesus of Nazareth*.)

This Jewish component of Wagner's symbolic investment in Siegmund brings up an important issue, an important reversal, in the history of nineteenth-century German-Jewish relations and symbolic constructions of selves and Others. The loading of Siegmund with a Jewish fantasy brings out not the phantasmagorical construction of the Jew as Other, but the obverse, fantastical construction of the Jew as innermost, and most dangerous, Self. As we know, the fantasmatic Other becomes most threatening when it seems to embody the innermost and most repressed aspects of the self.

Siegmund is thus the embodiment of a complicated and ambivalent Jewish fantasy. This fantasy is both philo-Semitic and anti-Semitic—two postures which also turn out to be more alike than different. Siegmund is a noble outsider and also, if we believe Fricka, a defiler of community and a seducer. He is a complicated character, and taking his name in vain can be treacherous.

The young Thomas Mann—aesthetically precocious and ideologically confused—fell head first into the maelstrom of the fin-de-siècle fantasy of the Jewish Siegmund. In his 1905 story "The Blood of the Walsungs," Mann portrayed a hard-working Teuton named Beckerath, a cultural philistine engaged to the highly refined Sieglinde Aarenhold, whose primary loyalty is to her twin brother, Siegmund. Beckerath is Hunding and Mann himself, and Sieglinde of course holds the position of Katia Pringsheim, twin sister of Klaus, Mann's wife, whom he married that same year, and whose family were not pleased by this story. We should not be pleased with it either, because its equation of Jewishness with racial separateness and incest is so clear that it has no need to be explicit.

The story opens at an afternoon dinner chez Aarenhold, at which Siegmund and Sieglinde ask Beckerath if he will permit the brother and sister to attend a performance of *Die Walküre* that evening as a last act of sibling intimacy before Sieglinde's wedding. The two hear the performance alone in the family's box. Mann then narrates the plot of *Die Walküre*, as witnessed by the twins.

> Siegmund gave a moving account of the hatred and envy which had been the bane of his life and his strange father's life, how their hall had been burnt, his sister carried off, how they had led in the forest a harried, persecuted, outlawed life; and how finally he had mysteriously lost

his father as well. And then Siegmund sang the most painful thing of all: he told of his yearning for human beings, his longing and ceaseless loneliness. He sang of men and women, of friendship and love he had sometimes won, only to be thrust back again into the dark. A curse had lain upon him forever, he was marked by the brand of his strange origins.[2]

The erotic charge between Siegmund and Sieglinde Aarenhold increases through the performance, and when they return home, they not only consummate their love just like their Wagnerian models, but they do it on a bearskin. Mann closes the story with the observation that, in Siegmund Aarenhold's postcoital agitation, "for a second the marks of his race stood out strong upon his face." Racial Jewishness can no longer be concealed, Mann tells us, in the natural, bearskin state of incestuous sex. Accusations of renegade or hyper male sexuality have continued to accompany racist tropes, including those of U.S. skin color–based racism and of Islamophobia.

The anti-Semitism in Mann's portrayal should not obscure the equally strong proclivity of German Jewish audiences to identify with Siegmund. Fin-de-siècle Jewish audiences certainly caught the sting of the stereotyping in Alberich, Mime, and, more subtly, Loge. But just as certainly they did not identify with these characters. If they accepted the anti-Semitic stereotype, they are more likely to have identified with the producer of the stereotype and connected these characters with their idea of culturally inferior Eastern European Jewry. They identified with Siegmund and named their sons after him. Like Lohengrin's, Siegmund's origins are noble but irrelevant to his position in the outside world; his heroism was self-produced, as was his personality in general.

Indeed, that inner identification continued past 1933. Ernst Bloch wrote that Siegmund and Sieglinde must be understood as refugees, as the love motif expresses a profound solitude. Siegmund, Bloch says, comports himself as the most lucid, the most free, and the least conformist of all the heroes of the *Ring*, completely different from the "free" Siegfried, who remains content to follow ingenuously his own nature.[3]

It is worth noting a significant return of a passionate, possibly eroticized, but not really incestuous brother-sister pair in Richard Strauss and Hugo von Hofmannsthal's opera *Elektra* (1909). The reunion and alliance of Elektra and Orestes is anchored in their shared desire for revenge and matricide: the avenging of the murder of their father, Agamemnon, by their mother,

Clytemnestra, after he sacrificed their sister, Iphigenia, at the start of the war against Troy. The scene of their mutual nonrecognition and then recognition, followed by Elektra's confession of shame in front of her brother ("O lass deine Augen nicht sehen ..."), proceeds with a strongly Wagnerian orchestral palette and passion, combined with a vocal line reminiscent of Isolde's lament over the dead Tristan. This late return of the brother-sister pair doesn't undermine Sabean's historicization of the trope to an earlier period. Rather, it supports it through the different way in which it exposes the social nonviability of the incestuous couple. Siegmund and Sieglinde's union is imagined by their socially transgressive father, Wotan, as an instrument for the repossession of the future—literally the eventual victory of the half-mortal breed of the Volsungs against the insurgent power of the Nibelungs. That plan is scuttled by Fricka in her dual role of marriage goddess and defender of contractual and bourgeois order. In social and structural terms, their union marks a failed beginning and the ardent but failed hope of restoring both the nobility and beauty of society as well as the reconciliation of society and desire: civilization without discontents, so to speak. Virtually every telling of the story of Elektra and Orestes places their reunion into a hopeless endgame of both social order and emotional satisfaction. There is no hope that their revenge and matricide—fulfilled as they are—will prove restorative to either register. In the Strauss-Hofmannsthal telling, after Sophocles, they are banished to disappearance from the stage (Orestes) and death (Elektra).

3. Politics of Listening

The prelude to act 1 of *Die Walküre* had scene-painted a storm through which Siegmund ran before stumbling into Sieglinde and Hunding's hut. The prelude to act 2 is more abstract in its imposition of violence; even so, variations of the sword motif persist through both preludes and make close siblings of them. The act 2 prelude opens with a reiteration (no longer an iteration) of the sword motif, again in the trumpet and again in the clarion key of C major, while the orchestra beneath it pulls down to the relative A minor. Indeed there is a kind of supplementary heaviness in this orchestral moment. It moves swiftly through quotations of some of the most rapturous phrases of Sieglinde's recognition of Siegmund in act 1 (which will become the music of her exhaustion and anguish in act 2) to the introduction of Brünnhilde and her equestrian theme. This theme, later to become the "Ride of the Valkyries" theme, corresponds at the opening of act 2 to Brünnhilde's carefree devotion to Wotan. Music drama seems to admonish here, as the prelude's articulation of the theme is preceded by eight bars of exaggeratedly heavy dotted rhythm, as if to introduce an unexplained heaviness in the music's (and Brünnhilde's) gait. Perhaps instinctively, Barenboim conducts these bars with a distinct ritardando. This music becomes metaphorical, suggesting the overtaking of the transgressive son, Siegmund, by the punishing father, Wotan, which is the traumatic reversal of generational inheritance.

We are introduced to Wotan and Brünnhilde in their fleeting moment of easy confidence and unconflicted alliance as Wotan instructs his daughter to assure Siegmund's victory against Hunding. This basically trivial exchange is followed by Wotan and Fricka alone: one of the most grinding marital dialogues on the opera stage, rivaled perhaps only by those between Verdi's Macbeth pair and by Wotan and Erda in act 3 of *Siegfried*. Defending marriage against both adultery and incest with every social and cultural rule supporting her, Fricka has cathected not only to Hunding himself but to the letter *h*. "Der Ehe Hüterin hörte ihn" (The guardian of marriage heard him), she tells Wotan. Wotan's tactics are condescending and formulaic. First he seeks Fricka's alliance in the service of the pure love between Siegmund and Sieglinde. When that fails, he insults her imagination: "Stets gewohntes magst du verstehn" (You understand only the ordinary). Finally, all his loopholes close: Siegmund's sword is magical, he claims; he controls the magic, she counters. Brünnhilde is autonomous, he pleads; she remains subject to his order, Fricka checkmates.

Careless staging of this scene can render Fricka a nuisance. August Everding's Chicago *Walküre* (1996) offered a delightful and almost comic performance by Marjana Lipovšek as an equestrian dominatrix with a riding crop in hand, but the absence of pathos rendered the scene at once enjoyable and banal. More insightful options emphasize Fricka's emotional and indeed erotic authority over Wotan, in addition to her invocation of social norms. Whereas Chéreau had emphasized the couple's continuing physical and erotic intimacy, at Bayreuth in the early 1990s Harry Kupfer gave greater weight to Wotan's continuing emotional dependence on Fricka. I frankly don't recall the Scala-Berlin performances of this scene ever achieving comparable precision. The two Wotans (Vitaly Kovalyov and René Pape) remained blunt, while Ekaterina Gubanova did not match her sonic near-perfection with a parallel emotional or dramatic range of subtlety.

Fricka's defeat of Wotan's plan is clinched by his oath to obey her, and his oath is followed by a slow eight-bar phrase that Alex Ross labeled a mini-interlude, or "microlude." Its rising phrase appears bogged down by increasing chromaticism, limited to half-step elevations before being overtaken by a theme associated with the suffering of the Volsungs. Barenboim conducts this passage with stately deliberateness. Ross asserted that the magic of these bars accrues from their liberation from leitmotivic material. This is not correct; nevertheless, his instinct to *hear* the leitmotivic phrases as imprecise or nonsignifying material is most welcome. We can give these ten bars multiple associations: as the orchestra's and music drama's sympathy for Wotan, as Wotan's inner eulogy for the Volsungs and for the son he is about to kill, as the death of a marriage. Wotan's motivation disappears just minutes after his introduction into the drama—a fact that the duration of his decline can easily obscure. The end of his marriage, despite his history of infidelity, must be understood as an element of his demoralization, despite the bitterness of the conflict that undoes both it and him.

The Wotan-Fricka scene is the first of the three dialogues that fill this great act of the *Ring*. The second is the long scene between Wotan and Brünnhilde, in which he reneges on his support for Siegmund and orders her to assure the young man's death at the hand of Hunding. The third is the so-called *Todesverkündigung*, or announcement of death, in which Brünnhilde, carrying out an apparently routine assignment, appears to Siegmund as the Valkyrie announcing the hero's imminent mortal death and induction into Valhalla's roster of fallen heroes. Siegmund's refusal of this investiture amounts to a radical disavowal of oedipal authority on the part of Wotan's son Siegmund *and* his daughter Brünnhilde. Freud himself cited Siegmund's gesture as such.[4]

Act 2 of *Die Walküre* establishes the dramatic dialogue as the aesthetic, formal, and philosophical principle of the *Ring* and of Wagnerian music drama. In an important new study of musical form in the later Wagner (from the *Ring* through *Parsifal*), Karol Berger channels Dahlhaus's grounding of music drama in the principle and practice of dramatic dialogue. Dialogue is the key to music drama's self-removal from the category and practices of opera. At the same time, both Dahlhaus and Berger caution that Wagner, in Dahlhaus's words, "did not emancipate himself as completely as he believed" from the world of opera. Indeed, act 1 of *Die Walküre* is wonderfully operatic in its passions, declamations, and forms. Siegmund and Sieglinde's narratives take on recitative-aria forms ("Ein Schwert verhiess mir der Vater" and "Der Männer Sippe"), and they each have a second aria (Siegmund's "Winterstürme wichen dem Wonnemond" and Sieglinde's "Du bist der Lenz, nach dem ich verlangte"). To be sure, Wagner holds back on operatic expectations by refusing them a duet and by ending the act with a series of individual declamations. The operatic eros of act 1 of *Die Walküre* suggests that the lovers' second set of arias grounds them musically and erotically in the present moment; their ecstasy has no capacity for a past or a future. This is where Berger, following Dahlhaus, is so insightful about the argument of Wagnerian dialogue:

> The closed forms of vocal melody—the aria, the duet—tend to isolate the present from the past and future, and this isolation was precisely what the music drama wanted to overcome. Thus, what was needed was a new way to compose the recitative, a way that would preserve its "open" declamatory character and yet make it musically more substantial, and, most important, put these new musical means at the service of the drama: it is on them primarily that the burden of binding the present with its past and future was to rest. Indeed, in an entry in the *Diary* on January 12, 1873, Cosima Wagner noted her husband's remark: "That is my real innovation: that I have incorporated dialogue into opera, and not just as recitative."[5]

It is easy enough to imagine Wagner writing the text of the *Ring* from his Swiss exile, allegorizing the gods as the failed patriarchs of Europe's old regimes with the hope of renewal in a rebellious and iconoclastic new generation. In this sense the focus of the *Ring* is not its own long story but that which will come after it. However, the *Ring* becomes a tragic masterpiece—according to the principle of tragedy—when the future is foreclosed, in other words in act 2 of *Die Walküre*. It becomes a tragedy when music drama comes into its own: as a series of dialogues in which the past is revised and transformed by characters trying to negotiate their desires and their fates. Wagner's 1848 and its moment of political radicalism and aesthetic futurism fade not so much under the glare of conservatism and institutionalization—that will come later, with Bayreuth and *Parsifal*—but in the shadow of the maturation of music drama. It's art that undoes revolution, the art of psychological depth and nuance. These are formal aspects of music drama; they also come to be personified in the character of Wotan. Wagner winds up having too much sympathy for Wotan to want him to disappear from the musical or historical scene. Wotan's tragic grandeur is matched by an explored psychic interiority that has prompted many sympathetic listeners to compare the depths of characterization in the *Ring* to the textures of the nineteenth-century novel.[6]

Will Siegmund live or die? This is the "action item" driving all three act 2 dialogues. The future, specifically the future of the gods, will be contingent upon this decision. Wotan's reversal of his earlier command that Brünnhilde assure Siegmund's victory involves a long review of his predicament combined with a sustained affirmation of the intimacy between father and daughter. There is a notable recapitulation here of the evolving musical textures of act 1: the birth of intimacy through a musical minimalism that approaches complete silence, followed by an evolving reinscription of passion, now the passion of defeat and defeatism rather than of an erotic beginning. There is of course much more Wotan in this scene than Brünnhilde, so much so that the scene is almost always referred to as Wotan's monologue. But the point is a didactic one: Brünnhilde is *listening*, and closely (figs. 2.3 and 2.4).

She is Wotan's ideal audience, and Wagner's as well. This is the first evident step of her journey to wisdom: she is allowed into the doubts and contradictions of her father's life story, eager to learn from this intimacy. When Wotan accounts for the transparency of his disclosures to his daughter by alleging that, in speaking to her, he is speaking to himself, she responds with a reassurance that carries a fully translatable linguistic ambiguity:

> Zu Wotans Willen sprichst du,
> sagst du mir was du willst;
> Wer bin ich,
> wäre ich dein Wille nicht?
>
> Say to me what you will:
> You are speaking to Wotan's will.
> Who am I,
> If not your will?

Brünnhilde's utterance carries its own contradiction: "say what you will" means both "tell me your true will (that Siegmund should live) and "say what you will" (that he should die)—and I will still know what you truly desire. In their long, final conversation in act 3, Brünnhilde will try, without success, to resolve the contradiction by citing Wotan's ambivalence—*Zwiespalt*—on the Siegmund question. The director's challenge—perhaps

FIG. 2.3. *Die Walküre*, act 2: Brünnhilde listens to Wotan. Photo: Koen Broos.

FIG. 2.4. *Die Walküre*, act 2: Brünnhilde. Photo: Koen Broos.

more difficult here than anywhere in the *Ring*—is to shape these long and beautiful dialogues as conversations rather than as situations, to direct through the text and its psychologically nuanced subtexts.

In act 2 Brünnhilde listens; in act 3 she argues back to Wotan. Yet here too they both clearly listen to each other. Wilhelmine patriarch that he is, Wotan refuses the distinction between authority and principle and remains steadfast in his punitive confidence. Yet he does alter the punishment significantly in ceding to Brünnhilde's plea that her sleep be broken only by a great hero, rather than by the first man who finds her. She also makes it clear to Wotan that this hero will be the son of Siegmund and Sieglinde, and by this point she has already instructed Sieglinde to name him Siegfried. Though Wotan professes uninterested contempt for the continuation of the

Volsungs' story, it is nevertheless clear to him, to Brünnhilde, and to us that she has persuaded him to allow the story to continue: the Volsungs' story, the ring's, and, however passively, the story of Wotan's desire to reclaim the ring as object and the *Ring* as story for his own purposes. From here on, and throughout the opera *Siegfried*, Wotan will struggle—somewhat incoherently—between agency and passivity, between *schaffen* and *schauen*, action and observation: the binary he will disingenuously present to Alberich in act 2 of *Siegfried*.

The act of listening that Brünnhilde's posture in act 2 exemplifies, together with its implicit allegorization of our own listening to Wotan, Wagner, and the *Ring*, marks the capacity of listening to rise to the level of active partnership in dialogue. This is a point of considerable importance to the formal texture and political meaning of music drama. Active listening is learning; learning is changing—the alteration or even transformation of the self. In the *Ring* as elsewhere, there are clear instances where formal texture makes it clear that a character is actively listening, learning, and changing. There are also instances of the opposite: moments where the character is *not* listening to evidence that we, the audience, are able to hear if in fact we ourselves are listening. When, for example, the curtain goes up on act 3 of *Die Meistersinger* to reveal a brooding, melancholy Hans Sachs, we can infer that he, like us, has been listening to the music of the prelude, nondiegetic as that music, for all intents and purposes, may be. In the great "Wahn" monologue that will soon follow, Sachs will articulate clearly and eloquently his will to understand and engage the flawed world around him, and he will do so to the music and motifs of the prelude. In a scenario that takes the opposite tack, when the self-deluding Isolde professes her contempt for Tristan (act 1), she is not listening to the orchestra's minor-key variation on the major-key love motif, which tells us what she is repressing, namely her love for Tristan.

The politics of active listening remain subtle. If active listening maintains the listener's silence, whether vis-à-vis another character (as in the case of Brünnhilde and Wotan) or vis-à-vis an implied narrative voice (as in the case of the Wagnerian orchestra and the examples of Hans Sachs and Isolde above), then the listener's silence may not be readily distinguishable from the acceptance of the speaker's authority. This ambiguity brings into relief the equities and inequities of the act of learning itself, of the relation between teacher and student, authority and apprentice, speaker and listener. Learning may be described as deferred equity, and indeed as the possibility for the student eventually to surpass the teacher.

The pathos of Siegmund's death has many dimensions. At bottom, it is an act of filicide. Filicide is in turn expandable into the generational violence of fathers against sons, including the potential of rulers to send sons too callously into battle. With more historical specificity, Siegmund's death must be heard as the lament for a century. For the historian and theorist Reinhart Koselleck, this is the "saddle century" from 1750 to 1850, from the Enlightenment through the Romantics. More narrowly, it is the death of revolutionary subjectivity and hope passed through the three generations from 1789 to 1848, and through the repetitions of revolution and reform followed by reaction and restoration. Closest to the moment, Siegmund's is the disappointed generation of 1848, accompanied by the programs of German liberalism and its hopes for a constitutional state. The failed revolutions of 1848 had in addition a pan-European mentality, the awareness that local and national insurgencies had regional and continental counterparts. In my student days the point of comparison and present-day relevance for the unsuccessful revolutions of 1848 were the similarly failed alliances between students and workers in the events of 1968. The abortive Arab Spring of 2011 and after appears to be today's even more unfortunate analog. The pan-European mentality of 1848 suffered an additional defeat in the post-1848 fading of transferable liberal structures into national and nationalist paradigms that by definition resisted internationalist attitudes.

Siegmund is a child of '48; Siegfried is a son of the Wilhelmine epoch, of the *Gründerzeit*, of empire. Siegfried achieves his majority in the summer of 1876. (It is worth noting that the German term for majority, *Mündigkeit*, is a variant of the word *Mund* [mouth]. Becoming an adult is held to be synonymous with having a voice in the public sphere.) If Siegfried first sings in 1876, we must infer that his father Siegmund met his death at the complicitous hand of his own father twenty years before. In truth, Siegmund first sang in Munich in the summer of 1870—a not insignificant date for the symbolic death of the generation of 1848. Whether early audiences of *Die Walküre* felt the resonance of such symbolism remains our guess.

Siegmund is the beloved subject not only of the story, but of music drama as a form. Musical subjectivity does not recover from this emplotted death. Siegmund's offspring, Siegfried, stands for an entirely new musical as well as political aesthetic, namely, the passage from free subjectivity to an imposed, restricted identity. There develops, in the opera *Siegfried*, a kind of symbiotic impoverishment of the character Siegfried and the formal delivery of music drama. The character is rigid, and the texture becomes so as well. As an opera, *Siegfried* remains, to my ear, deeply satisfying and successful, but in different ways, as the following chapter will argue. My argument here involves the fused political and formal exhaustion so abundantly evident in the generational passage from Siegmund to Siegfried and from *Die Walküre* to *Siegfried*. The *Ring* itself thus symptomatizes at the same time as it performs the death of a free and open subjectivity in the post-1848 generation.

Siegfried, we may recall, is the purely instrumental object of Wotan's scheme to regain the Ring and its power. Forced through contract and law to relinquish Alberich's Ring to the giant Fafner, Wotan must create a "free agent" who will repossess the fetish object with no knowledge that he is working for his own family business. In Wotan's imagination, Siegfried is a thing, not a person. It is Siegmund whom Wotan loves—and kills; Siegmund who is the mid-century bourgeois son in this fundamentally bourgeois epic of a social, industrial, and politically climbing family.

In the generational passage from Siegmund to Siegfried, from 1848 to 1870, from liberal hope to nationalist power, the nineteenth century is lost. The death of Siegmund at the hand of his self-entrapped father, Wotan, offers a brutal allegory of the destruction of subjectivity at the hand of a self-entrapped modernity, where rationality has produced not freedom but Max Weber's iron cage. In directing Brünnhilde to assure Siegmund's death, Wotan not only sacrifices his son but also betrays himself. In disinheriting Brünnhilde for her transgression, wherein she obeys his inner will rather than his revised order, Wotan encloses himself in a punitive patriarchal rigidity that relies on a culture of punishment. The pathos of Wotan's Farewell at the conclusion of *Die Walküre* resides in its overdetermination: it is Wotan's farewell to a promise of subjectivity that he has never understood and that he has failed because of his own arrogance; it is at some level Wagner's farewell to a world that he has similarly failed; it is thus at some level a farewell to music. As Brünnhilde tells Wotan, he has become his own enemy, a predicament that is also Wagner's and music drama's.

THREE

Bad Education

1. Music Drama and the Unconscious

*S*IEGFRIED, THE THIRD EVENING OF *DER RING DES NIBELUNGEN* (the second if we label *Das Rheingold* as a prologue or *Vorabend*—literally a pre-evening—as Wagner did), is often referred to as the tetralogy's scherzo. A certain levity runs through it, no doubt supplied mostly by the boyish, guileless Siegfried himself, by his fleeting companion the Forest Bird, and by his ultimate discovery and sexual conquest of Brünnhilde, the resolution that marks the work as a comedy in the classical sense. Yet a very slight change of perspective reveals *Siegfried* as the darkest of the four works.

The darkness of the opera's visual landscape—from the dingy lair of act 1 through the impenetrable forest of act 2 (every guidebook will remark how uniquely dense and light deprived are German forests, a reality affirmed by both folklore and the Brothers Grimm) through the abject, nocturnal exchange between Wotan and Erda in act 3—gives way only at the end to the blazing light of Siegfried's awakening of Brünnhilde. There is a vocal darkness in play as well; the voices are all male until the Forest Bird chirps briefly in act 2. The forest's direst dangers are human and emotional. Here both Siegmund and Sieglinde have died, unsheltered and unprotected, and here Siegfried has endured a miserable childhood, confined by Mime's claustrophobic hut and malevolent surveillance: the setting of act 1. Act 2 is set deeper in the forest, at the place even Wotan fears (according to the Valkyries): the dragon Fafner's pit. And the dark mountain pass of act 3 becomes the place of Wotan's final emotional and political defeat: first by Erda, then by Siegfried.

At the opera's midpoint, at the terrifying black hole of Fafner's lair, Siegfried relaxes. He has no knowledge of the world and its dangers; he therefore has no fear. Knowledge and fear are identical here, in the same way that love and death are in *Tristan und Isolde*. But at this moment in the *Ring*—the long day of the action of *Siegfried*—no one has knowledge.

Here lies the work's real darkness. We are truly in the shadow of Greek tragedy, where the gods themselves have no knowledge, no understanding of the world. Cassiers and Bagnoli's set for the act 2 forest again projects indecipherable messages onto the tubular trees, mesmerizing us with nature's opaque codes and unreadability. The *Ring* itself, and especially a post-Anthropocene *Ring* such as this one, is all about the tragedy of human disrespect for the natural world. Speaking directly with nature remains a function of magic and possibly of psychosis, and certainly a further symptom of such disrespect.

Where knowledge has gone dark, no one learns and no one teaches. Or, more accurately, the schools are bad and the education is worthless. There can be no good answers to bad questions, and *Siegfried* is all about bad questions: Mime's to Wotan and then Wotan's to Mime in act 1, Wotan's to Erda and then to Siegfried in act 3. All of these bad teachers ratify Siegfried's complaint to Mime about his bad education, about the lack of both teaching and learning (*lehren* and *lernen*) in this dreary home school:

> Vieles lehrtest Du, Mime,
> Und manches lernt' ich von Dir;
> Doch was Du am liebsten mich lehrtest,
> zu lernen gelang mir nie:
> wie ich Dich leiden könnt'.
>
> You have taught much, Mime,
> And I have learned a few things from you;
> But what you most wanted to teach me
> I was never able to learn:
> How to stomach you!

Unredeemable brute though he may be, Siegfried has earned his contempt for Mime as parent and teacher. In Chicago in 1995-96, John Conklin peppered Mime's lair with tiny, precious pieces of furniture—chairs and tables that would always have been too small for Siegfried and thus only markers of Mime's obsequiousness and condescension. Like legions of bad teachers, and so many Wilhelmine parents, Mime has drummed conventions into the boy, rather than understanding guidance as an invitation to formation. In the broad categories of nineteenth-century Germany, this pattern follows the cultural and ideological displacement of *Bildung* by *Besitz*: aesthetic education by property and possession as the national priority. Deploying these categories, Jürgen Habermas divided the century into two periods, with 1860 as dividing line. We will return to this thesis, but in the meantime we can assert that education as cultivation always risks devolving into the transmission of fixed elements of ownable, brandable knowledge, or into the confusion of knowledge and information.[1]

Siegfried does appear to have inherited one attractive trait from his father here: a penchant for the letter *l*. Recall Siegmund's

> Winterstürme wichen dem Wonnemond,
> in mildem Lichte leuchtet der Lenz; —
> auf linden Lüften leicht und lieblich,
> Wunder webend er sich wiegt. . . .

According to Wagner's codes of consonant rhyme (*Stabreim*) and of allegedly musical and unmusical, pleasing and ugly consonants (Siegmund's *w*'s and *l*'s versus Alberich's hard *g*'s), Siegfried shows here some unconscious potential for musicality and the knowledge it brings. This knowledge is both cognitive and — since it is born of the beauty of sound — sensual. It follows, then, that he will receive both a cognitive and a sensual education from Brünnhilde. (The one kind of education that he will receive only with catastrophic delay from Brünnhilde is a musical one, as will become evident at the moment of his undoing in act 2 of *Götterdämmerung* and, with significant musical and cognitive difference, at the moment of his death in act 3.)

Following the aesthetic that matured decisively in the first two acts of *Die Walküre*, *Siegfried* proceeds also by way of intimate conversations and pained recollections. First, Mime laments that he himself has know-how — technique (*techne*) — but no knowledge. He can make swords but cannot reforge *the* sword, Nothung, the weapon that shattered upon Siegmund's betrayal and murder. Next, Siegfried complains about his own lack of learning. Finally, Wotan and Mime waste each other's time. Here we have an important question about what Wotan is up to.

In act 2, scene 1, Wotan ("the Wanderer") declares to his nemesis, Alberich, and to the audience, "Zu schauen kam ich, nicht zu schaffen" (I have come to look, not to act). But we have no way of knowing whether he is sincere or not. Perhaps he has come to unnerve Mime and thus to free Siegfried — in other words, to relaunch his original scheme of regaining the Ring without legally breaking his deal with Fafner, the survivor of the two brother giants. This motive is a plausible one in light of the three riddles he poses to the harassed Mime. When Mime is unable to answer the third one, unable to say who will reforge the magic sword, Wotan reveals that the task will be achieved only by one who does not know fear. No doubt this move is designed to prompt Mime to test Siegfried, to spur him to remake his father's sword and to use it. In the subsequent, highly static interview, Mime does try to test Siegfried's immunity to fear. But this element is largely superfluous, as it is clear that Mime's motive in raising Siegfried has been all along the wish to indenture the boy as the agent who will seize Fafner's hoard for Mime himself. In any case, Wotan does certainly succeed in unnerving Mime, driving him finally to state flat-out to Siegfried that he intends to kill him. Wotan destabilizes Alberich as well, suggesting that Mime will be his only rival in winning the Ring from Fafner, as Siegfried has no knowledge of it or its power. Next, he awakens Fafner for no apparent reason, as he will also do with Erda, a far more interesting interlocutor, at the start of act 3. Wotan appears to be Alberich's equal in this scene, reduced to the same level of vulgarity and inefficacy. With the exception of one swelling phrase in which Valhalla is invoked, Wotan's music also betrays a state of deterioration. Whether Wagner is himself in control here or not also remains a question. He may be defanging the god's music along with the god himself—just as Shakespeare was capable of writing uninspired verse for characters as an indication of their over- or underinflated status. Even the most fervent Wagnerites will usually admit that the music and music drama in act 2 of *Siegfried* suffer a considerable loss of momentum. According to this view—rendered all the more understandable by the tendency of act 2 of *Siegfried* to wilt in performance—the *Ring* seems to have required the long break that delayed the composition of act 3.

So conventional wisdom would have it. Indeed, the pace is slow here and the sequencing of scenes problematic. Who has patience for another round of the gnawing bickering between Alberich and Mime as they scamper onto the stage following the satisfying scene between Siegfried and Fafner, who is given a moment of noble pathos before dying? At the same time, however, there is a kind of nobility about the very aimlessness and structural unpredictability of act 2, as if the awakening of the unconscious were receiving acknowledgment by the nod to formlessness. The act 2 prelude, with its brooding and menace that give way to a threat or at least an insistence in the percussion, describes Fafner's black hole and at the same time introduces the act as the black hole at the center of the *Ring* itself. Music drama confesses here, one might suggest, to its ultimate lack of knowledge and control, including self-control. The same effect is produced by the act's openness to nature and its artlessness. Rather than assuming that this the *Ring*'s destructive act, we might give some room to the possibility that the second act of *Siegfried* is the *Ring*'s deconstructive act: interested in the instability and multiplicity of meaning at the levels of both story and form.

The Forest Murmurs scene finds Siegfried lying supine on the forest floor, at once passive and alert to what he might learn. The moment encloses both Siegfried and us into a mode and mood in which Debussy might have been comfortable. *Pelléas et Mélisande* starts in this kind of place and, unlike the opera *Siegfried* and the *Ring* itself, never leaves it. *Pelléas*'s modernism lodges on the spectrum between late Wagner and Samuel Beckett. Act 2 of *Siegfried* finds its place earlier on the same spectrum, even though Wagner's musical texture here offers a less flexible guide.

Cassiers and Bagnoli's set for act 1 of *Siegfried* consists of steel gratings formed into a series of full or partial cubes. Abstract only up to a point, the space also suggests an industrialized workshop or metal shop of some kind. The proscenium is framed by an archway formed of steel fragments, which we come to discern as a maze of discarded swords. Someone here—Mime, we surmise—has been trying and failing to forge a sword. Mime's opening lament to that effect is interrupted by Siegfried, who enters, according to Wagner's stage directions, leading a wild bear. In this production the bear is a full-sized pelt that Siegfried has thrown over his shoulders like a cape. Consider here the following passage from Bruce Chatwin's *Songlines*:

> Among the military fraternities of Ancient Germany a young man, as part of his training to stifle inhibitions against killing, was required to strip naked; to dress himself in the hot, freshly flayed skin of a bear; to work himself into a "bestial" rage: in other words, to go, quite literally, berserk.
>
> "Bearskin" and "berserk" are the same word. The helmets of the Royal Guards, on duty outside Buckingham Palace, are the descendants of this primitive battle costume.[2]

If "bearskin" and "berserk" are the same word, the mirroring posits a continuity, if not the very identity, of natural and human violence. At face value, Siegfried is an *enfant sauvage* tamed only by Mime's (bad) education. As a creation of Wagner and music drama, Siegfried combines innocence with a certain overdetermined brutality.

During the Mime-Wotan interview in act 1, the horizontal platform made of the steel square begins to rotate into a vertical backdrop with stairs, so that the space in which Siegfried finally forges the sword—the set's witty version of a teenager's locked upstairs bedroom—is located above Mime's workspace. Several of the steel grids, now vertical and therefore facing the audience, become screens on which various images of fire and firepower are projected. These accompany and illustrate the forging process, but not innocently. This brash, multitasking Siegfried forges his sword to apparently inspirational media images of firebombing and ruined cityscapes, suggesting the destructive potential of the power that the young hero reconstitutes so naively. The forging song that he sings while he works is not only itself *about* overblowing (via the bellows essential to the smithy); it is itself almost self-consciously overblown. Therein lies its pleasure, but indeed its guilty pleasure. Frankly, I always feel that my own delight in the Forging Song places and implicates me inside a musical analog to a beer-soaked Oktoberfest tent. Like the sword itself, the song becomes an invitation to violence. On the Cassiers-Bagnoli stage, Siegfried's induction into this violent potential is corroborated by the video screens—equipment, perhaps, of the protected adolescent, but in their supply of fantasy not unlike Alberich's highly mediatized power perch in scene 3 of *Das Rheingold* or the Gulf War–like projections behind the opening tableau of act 2 of *Die Walküre*.

The midpoint of act 2, a return to innocence, comes as Siegfried muses in the forest about his lost mother and his unhappy childhood with Mime. In some ways, this beautiful and mysterious moment at the act's center echoes the inner recollection and exploration of Wotan's act 2 monologue in *Die Walküre*. There, Wotan's self-absorption was overtaken by his capacity to learn from himself as he listened to himself, thereby imparting the art of listening to his daughter Brünnhilde. The art of listening, of education and self-education, does indeed involve the id's ceding some ground to the ego—as in Freud's motto "Wo Es war, soll Ich werden" (Where the id was, the ego shall be).[3] Unlike Wotan, Siegfried possesses little interiority and little capacity for self-analysis. Whereas Wotan somehow peers into the black hole of his unconscious, Siegfried doesn't develop the capacity to do so. The forest does open for Siegfried the possibility of a good education— an education that opens and respects a potentially autonomous subjectivity. He will arrive at this point suddenly and tragically at the moment of his death, in act 3 of *Götterdämmerung*. Now, unfortunately, his fearless personality suggests that there would be scant unconscious material for him to find there, in any case. He shares with both Parsifal and Tristan the longing to reexperience the moment of his birth and its association with his mother, who died during it. But unlike Tristan, to whom Wagner gave the time and pathos to build a portrait of a shattering and shattered ego, and unlike Parsifal, whom Wagner allowed to claim such maturity and knowledge without a convincing amount of inner work, Siegfried will evince comparable depth and knowledge only as he dies. Here, at the midpoint of what one might expect to amount to his *Bildungsoper*, the black hole of the unconscious is displaced onto nature and scenery, into the hole in the earth now inhabited by Fafner. This scenic displacement of the unconscious reveals all of the characters in this act—including Wotan—to be cut off from their own inner lives and thus from the capacity for either self-knowledge or knowledge of the world. Siegfried kills Fafner without any consideration of the act, while Fafner, rehumanized at the moment of death, dies nobly. Finally, Siegfried kills Mime with equal ignorance and insensitivity, though not without the justification of self-defense. Both acts of violence are banal; Siegfried kills, as Cassiers observed in a preproduction discussion, like a child playing a video game. (The televising of the Gulf War of 1990 rendered almost banal the hypothesis that adolescent video games had become the training ground for various forms of dehumanized warfare, such as drone piloting. As noted, Cassiers's inclusion of Gulf War-like images in *Die Walküre* is recapitulated in Siegfried's video screens and games.)

Fafner hasn't a clue, in his dogmatic slumber, what to do with the Ring, as he makes clear on awakening to Wotan's taunts and Alberich's fear: "Ich lieg' und besitz':—lasst mich schlafen!" (I rest and possess—let me sleep). Here again the signal category of *Besitz* is a virtual code word among German historians for the age of unification, empire building, and rapid industrialization that marked the 1870s, the decade of Germany's *Gründerzeit* or take-off period, and the decade of the 1876 premiere in Bayreuth of *Siegfried, Götterdämmerung*, and the complete *Ring*. The slogan of the period was *Bildung und Besitz*: education and possession, or "to know and to own." But, again, as many scholars have argued, Jürgen Habermas perhaps most famously (in his classic book *Strukturwandel der Öffentlichkeit* [*The Stuctural Transformation of the Public Sphere*]), Germany of the *Gründerzeit* can be better understood in terms of the replacement of *Bildung* by *Besitz*: a shift in values in which capital outpaced culture as the society's most prized property. (The word "property" itself incorporates the ambiguity between possession and characteristic.) Thus the early decades of the nineteenth century stand as periods of experimental politics, embattled liberalism, and cultural growth. *Bildung* becomes here the set of ideals bequeathed to the emerging bourgeoisie by the poets—Goethe above all—attaching the cultivation of the self to the building of society. There is an optimism in this formulation, in the potential compatibility of self- and social cultivation—the Age of Siegmund, one might say. The fin-de-siècle arrival of psychoanalysis as a paradigm of self-cultivation displaces *Bildung* in positing a basic competition between individuality and society. This is psychoanalysis's legacy of pessimistic liberalism—the voice, for example, of John Stuart Mill, whom the young Sigmund Freud translated. For the intervening generations, those of 1870 and the decades around unification—the Age of Siegfried— the consolidation and ever more rigid intensification of national, industrial, and imperial power championed *Besitz*, what today we call consumerism. And the presence of consumerism, the language of the client and the product, has of course made its way into higher education.

George Bernard Shaw, Joachim Herz, and Patrice Chéreau all placed the *Ring* into the decades of the German *Gründerzeit* with this context in mind. Fafner—quite unlike the Krupps, Thyssens, and Siemenses, as indeed the Rathenaus as well—proves quite incompetent as an industrial capitalist: he seems to have skipped that phase and jumped straight to consumerism. In his ignorance and literal sleepiness, he only hoards, failing entirely to participate in the new political economy of take-off capitalization.

Siegfried, as ignorant as Fafner about the art and power of the Ring, is no more interested in *Besitz* than he is, at least at this point in the story, in *Bildung*. He slays the dragon. But what is the dragon all about? Its terror lies in the mysteries of depth—what is invisible, what lies beneath, to borrow a phrase from Hollywood. Indeed, Hollywood's best version of the dragon may be the great white shark of the film *Jaws* (1975). If you are swimming in shark-infested waters, it is reasonable to fear sharks. But if you are terrified by the movie, then you are not literally afraid of the shark (which, notwithstanding the realism of the screen, is not real), but rather of what the shark represents: an attack from the impenetrable depths of your own person, from the unconscious. This is not fear but anxiety. Or rather, anxiety, as Freud argued, is fear without an object of fear, which turns into the fear of the self. Indeed, Wagner's dragon—unbeknownst to Siegfried himself—is invested with exactly this power. That terror should be communicated to the audience, à la *Jaws*: not an easy task. It helps that Wagner's dragon is principally a musical idea, not a visual one. The chromatic, minor-chord modulations that constitute the so-called dragon or Fafner motif resemble the so-called Ring motif itself. (I say "so-called" as a reminder of the destabilization of the leitmotif and its signifying capacities that I argued for in the introduction.)[4]

These dragon sounds do return to haunt Siegfried, in an excellent ex-

EX. 001. Ring

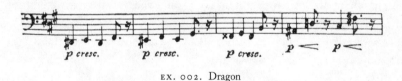

EX. 002. Dragon

ample of the return of a repressed memory at a moment of danger. They return when Siegfried finally learns fear—that is, at the moment he discovers Brünnhilde. It is difficult to banish the idea that Wagner is inserting a musical joke here. But the point is really not that the lady is a dragon. It is, rather, that Siegfried begins to show signs of a sense of self, history, knowledge, and anxiety at the moment of erotic discovery and its inscription of an unconscious. The elements shared by Brünnhilde and Fafner involve the descent into the unconscious and the pursuit and power of erotic knowledge. Eros then emerges as that aspect of the unconscious available to the mind and body, the foundation of the person's negotiation with the world. How to stage Siegfried's confrontation with the dragon convincingly as a battle of concrete bodies combined with the abstract threat of psychic terror is a challenge. Fritz Lang's ferocious phallus remains the model. Cassiers's solution of a billowing scarf dance did not succeed.

Siegfried's first experience of a female voice—and ours too, in the context of this opera—is delivered by the Forest Bird. This creature occupies an interesting position as an agent of transition, specifically the transition into a gendered human world. (Siegfried already knows that the animal world is gendered; on this basis he rejected Mime's claim to be at once father and mother to him.) The bird also guides the transition from natural sound (birdsong) to language and human song through the conceit that the tasting of the dragon's blood allows Siegfried to understand what the bird has to say. She has important things to tell him: first, that Mime intends to kill him, and second, that Brünnhilde, asleep on a rock, is his to awaken. The bird herself participates in the awakening of drive and eros in Siegfried, and thus the transition in his own associations from his unknown mother to his future lover.

Cassiers chose to literalize the feminine and eroticizing aura of the Forest Bird by having her appear onstage in the form of a nubile young woman whose silent gestures guide Siegfried to follow the bird, though she herself, as its human emanation, remains invisible to him. The doubling of the sonic Forest Bird with the visual presence (to the audience) of an icon of seductive femininity compounds their joint tutelage of Siegfried in his task to *chercher la femme*. Obedient to the fact that "he has never seen a woman before" (in Anna Russell's words) when he first encounters Brünnhilde, Siegfried has begun to learn a subliminal lesson through his strange encounter with the Forest Bird. Later on, when the intrigues of *Götterdämmerung* impair his cognition, this moment of his prediscovery of eros will form some part of his archive of subliminal knowledge.

He is a slow learner. Brünnhilde's awakening scene is ecstatic, to be sure. And her lament over the loss of her godliness and the impending loss of her virginity—"Ewig war ich"—is musically exquisite, a fitting basis for the lovely *Siegfried Idyll* that Wagner wrote for chamber orchestra and presented to his wife, Cosima, as a birthday gift. It also exudes a kind of Biedermeier chastity that is in keeping not only with Wagner's birthday gesture to his wife but also with the fact that, in placing the consummation of Siegfried and Brünnhilde's sexual relationship far earlier in the story than was the case in previous versions—prior to the encounter with the Gibichungs—Wagner is giving the terminally confused components of Siegfried's history of sexual encounters and (in)fidelities the distinct benefit of the doubt. As Wendy Doniger has written, Siegfried's sexual history is fused with his textual history. The *Ring*'s medieval source materials—the thirteenth-century Norse *Thidrekssaga*, Icelandic *Volsungasaga*, and Middle High German *Nibelungenlied*—agree despite variations that Siegfried either seduces or rapes Brünnhilde following his encounter with Gutrune.[5] In Wagner's version,

Siegfried does little more than insist. Hardly a skilled seducer, he—like the Flying Dutchman before him—merely claims and occupies the position, the *idée fixe*, that an obsessed woman has been reserving for him. Knowledge—erotic or other—will bring Siegfried death, not power. To be sure, the plot of *Götterdämmerung*, involving Siegfried's unwitting betrayal of Brünnhilde, depends on his forgetting of the third act of *Siegfried* by means of a potion. But Wagner concocted this potion of forgetfulness several years after he devised the love potion imbibed by Tristan and Isolde. In the case of *Tristan*, we are informed by the orchestra that the love potion is a kind of placebo, a pretext for the two characters' recognition—id become ego—of the intense forbidden love that has long existed between them. Siegfried's potion is pharmacologically similar but psychologically different. He forgets the previous plot in his story, but he has not apparently learned or internalized anything worth remembering; his own psychic depth arrives, as I have pointed out, only at the moment of his death.

Of the three dialogues that constitute act 3 of *Siegfried*, the one between Wotan and Erda exudes the most pathos. Here we have not new love but old love, the love associated with a long and embattled partnership, with interdependencies and intimacies both positive and negative. The first of act 3's three scenes, each one a dialogue (between Wotan and Erda, between Wotan and Siegfried, and between Siegfried and Brünnhilde), this one follows a newly energized and thickly scored orchestral prelude, reminiscent of the prelude to act 2 of *Die Walküre* but now oddly positive and optimistic in its reliance on the upward surges of the Rhine-earth-nature-Erda motivic cluster. When compared with the closely related preludes to acts 1 and 2 of *Siegfried*, the prelude to act 3 seems to release energies previously repressed, energies that in the previous two preludes were identified in the lower orchestra and associated with creatures of darkness: the dragon, dwarves, curses. These kinds of preludes regularly encourage directors to raise the curtain and accompany the orchestra with a staged (or, recently, filmed) pantomime. Barenboim rigidly resists and forbids such a move, arguing that the orchestra has exclusive rights to storytelling at such junctures. In my own experience, one decision has successfully overruled this principle: Pierre Audi's idea (Amsterdam, 1998) to have Wotan and Erda act out forty years of intimacy and strife, attraction and repulsion, through an ambulatory embrace and/or struggle that filled and expanded the moments of the act 3 prelude into a stunning history of intimacy and intimate violence.

Here again Wotan operates irrationally, with no discernible motivation.

Wake up! he commands his lover of forty years. Awake "aus wissendem Schlaf" (from knowing sleep)! But an epistemic gap separates these two figures and confounds their conversation. Erda's knowledge is that of principles, while Wotan seeks the clarification of events. Of unfolding events he already knows more than she. She refers him to her daughters, the Norns; presumably he already knows what we will soon witness, which is that their narration and authority have been broken. (The Norns will only occupy the stage in the prologue to *Götterdämmerung*, and the rope with which they narrate the course of the world will break only at the conclusion of that scene. But the temporality of that scene is indeterminate. The breakdown of narration, authority, and coherence is the plot of the *Ring* as a whole. The great scene of the Norns can therefore be understood as an overlay covering the full life of the tetralogy. It could in fact be played at the start of the *Ring*, before the actions of *Das Rheingold*. Except for brief references to Alberich's theft of the gold and Loge's lighting of Brünnhilde's rock, their narration focuses on the prehistory of the *Ring*'s story and action.) Erda then recommends Brünnhilde as a source of information, unaware of her fate since the end of *Die Walküre* and infuriated when she learns it.

Wotan changes the nature of his question to Erda, perhaps revealing more sincerely his motive in awakening her. What he now wishes to know is, "Wie besiegt die Sorge der Gott?" The question's syntax is economical and poetic. It relies in a completely ordinary manner on the German language's case structure and thus on the declension of the definite articles to reverse the object and subject of the sentence (how conquers anxiety [object] the god [subject]?). However, the feminine article *die* (in *die Sorge*) in the accusative is identical to that in the nominative, meaning that, as the question unfolds, the case of *die Sorge* is indeterminate. It becomes the grammatical object of the sentence only when the male nominative article *der* (in *der Gott*) claims its position as the marker of the subject. (If *Sorge* had remained the subject, then the accusative article *den* would have marked "the god" [*den Gott*] as the object. The thought would then read: how does anxiety conquer the god? No matter: its perfectly ordinary syntax and grammatical capacities notwithstanding, the sentence launches an instability of subject and object that is both syntactic and psychoanalytic. The god cannot master anxiety; anxiety has mastered the god. "How does the god master anxiety?" has become interchangeable with "How has anxiety mastered the god?"

To his question Erda has no answer. Go back to sleep, Wotan commands—to *eternal* sleep. It is difficult to parse the level of violence contained in this command. There is a special poignancy in the possibility that Wotan's story ends here—at the final breakdown of dialogue with the partner to whom he has been most intimately cathected, both erotically and intellectually. His misery is dire. Wotan, unlike Alberich, has never yet given up on love, so his renunciation of Erda assures his emotional demise, rendering almost trivial, by comparison, his loss of power in the scene with Siegfried that will follow apace. But Wotan's story and actions contain equally dire precedents of mixing love with violence. He murdered Siegmund, and he discarded Brünnhilde. (Recall that early concept discussion in Berlin, in which Jürgen Flimm offered a contemporary analog to Wotan's placement of Brünnhilde on her sleeping rock which I found precise and convincing: Wotan, Flimm suggested, proposes abandoning his daughter to the gutter, making a whore out of her and delivering her to any random sexual assault of the street.)

The demigoddess and woman Erda stands of course as an allegory for the earth—*die Erde*. The Cassiers production emphasized throughout that the violence of the gods entails a violence to the earth, a degradation of the environment. Wotan's violence to Erda thus stands as a summary, a recapitulation, of the violence of his regime to the earth in general. (Willa Cather writes, in *Death Comes for the Archbishop*: "In the working of silver or ... turquoise the Indians had exhaustless patience; upon their blankets and belts and ceremonial robes they lavished their skill and pains. But their conception of decoration did not extend to the landscape. They seemed to have none of the European's desire to 'master' nature, to arrange and re-create. ... It was as if the great country were asleep, and they wished to carry on their lives without awakening it.")

I suggested earlier that Cassiers's *Ring* takes place in the Anthropocene era and our awareness of the damage humans have created in the earth. How to affirm Wotan's violence in this scene, both to Erda and to *die Erde*? At this juncture of Cassiers's *Ring*, I found myself confounded by the difficulty of the scene and the feeling that its staging, no matter how elusive, was not receiving adequate inspiration. I began to wonder about a radical move that would do justice to the scene of violence against both earth and Woman, Erde and Erda. I wondered whether a decisive dramatic and political truth would be told by a production that would have Wotan kill Erda at the end of this ultimate scene of tragically failed intimacy, understood for the twenty-first century also in the context of environmental degradation. Such a move would show Wotan for who he can be, reminding the audience of as much in anticipation of his scene with Siegfried, when the dignified senior citizen, faced with the young thug's vulgarity, can too easily hold the higher moral ground. Wotan's murder of Erda would shock the audience, and one dramaturgical argument against it would attend to the possible difficulty of their recovering in time for the two scenes that follow. An argument in its favor would stress the opportunity to inflect the following scenes—all the way through *Götterdämmerung*—both visually and dramatically with the double violence of human and earthly violence.

Wotan's encounter with Siegfried results in the shattering of his spear—the avenging, by means of the reforged sword Nothung, of Siegmund's murder. Wotan's swift disappearance from the scene confirms his irrelevance to the story. It finalizes what we have suspected from his very first appearance as the Wanderer: that his power, his authority, and, perhaps most pathetically, his knowledge have all failed. Power and knowledge are symbiotic; but the seeker of power has an entirely different relation to the world and to mortality than the seeker of knowledge.

When the great scholar and founder of the discipline of sociology Max Weber was invited to give two lectures at the University of Munich in 1917, he announced as his two titles "Politik als Beruf" (Politics as a Vocation) and "Wissenschaft als Beruf" (Science [or Scholarship] as a Vocation). The first principle of the scholar or scientist, Weber argued in the second lecture, is the recognition that all knowledge is fleeting, is indeed designed to be revised and replaced by succeeding generations. Knowledge cannot therefore hope to sustain its own power. The assured demise of the authority of the gods, who refuse Weber's principle, involves a collapse of epistemic authority. And here a much larger dimension of the problem opens, one that indeed remains unnoticed by most listeners to Wagner's *Ring*. As Wotan's epistemic authority fades, so does music drama's. The founding principle of music drama involves the claim that *the music knows*. The music tells the true story based on its own capacities for narration and self-analysis. Wagner's music achieves both these things through the formally interreferential system of the leitmotifs and the possible relation of the leitmotifs to extramusical representations. It does so as well through the adoption of a Beethovenian symphonic palette and the latter's capacity to trace in purely musical terms the life of a subject in time, apparently driving to a future while at the same time able to refer to and comment on its own past. As a result of these attributes, the music of music drama, Wagner claims, possesses knowledge and meaning. For this reason, music drama amounts to the very opposite, so Wagner claims, of opera, where energies and gestures are devoid of knowledge and meaning and therefore trapped in triviality. The collapse of music drama's epistemic authority—coeval as it is with the regime of the gods—suggests its modulation into its alleged opposite: namely, opera. Within the bounds of Wagnerian orthodoxy, this proposition is heretical. Outside such orthodoxy, where music drama and opera are not held in opposition to each other, it may signal a welcome release, even a liberation.

2. Music Drama's Unconscious

Siegfried and Brünnhilde have two love duets. The second—the second scene of the prologue to *Götterdämmerung*—is the greater one. Internally—internally to the drama—that greatness can be understood in terms of Brünnhilde's humanization and Siegfried's delayed education, both of which are achieved in erotic encounter. Their duets follow the rules of music drama. They don't sing together (in which case Wagner's words and their musical values would be obfuscated); rather, each waits for the other to finish before responding. (Tristan and Isolde tested the disobedience of these rules in 1865, eleven years before Siegfried and Brünnhilde sang in public.) Nevertheless, at the level of the work itself, these vocal encounters can be heard and understood as an invitation to synthesis—not only erotic and affective, but also musical and formal: in other words, as the desire for the passage or transcendence from music drama into opera. At the ecstatic conclusion of the *Götterdämmerung* love duet, both the character Siegfried and the music drama *Götterdämmerung* have embarked on a journey that they will take to their own hearts of darkness, to their operatic unconscious. In *Götterdämmerung* we discover something about the content of three unconsciouses: Siegfried's (love), Brünnhilde's (love, but also violence), and music drama's (opera).

Nietzsche may have been the first to understand the need for the operatic aesthetic as the necessary relief from the codes of music drama. But he understood it as an antidote rather than as an inner capacity or desire—the health of the south as opposed to the sickliness of the north. The refinement of the French, he wrote in *Beyond Good and Evil* (1886), enabled them to appreciate "the south in the north and the north in the south.... It was for them that *Bizet* made music, this last genius to see a new beauty and seduction—who discovered a piece of *the south of music*.[6] A dozen years later, George Bernard Shaw's *Perfect Wagnerite* argued for music drama's reversal into opera. Despite his mischaracterization of the musical form of the second Siegfried-Brünnhilde duet, his general argument bears citing at some length:

> And now, O Nibelungen Spectator, pluck up; for all allegories come to an end somewhere; and the hour of your release from these explanations is at hand. The rest of what you are going to see is opera, and nothing but opera. Before many bars have been played, Siegfried and the wakened Brynhild, newly become tenor and soprano, will sing a concerted cadenza; plunge on from that to a magnificent love duet; and end with a precipitous allegro a capella, driven headlong to its end by the impetuous semiquaver triplets of the famous finales to the first act of Don Giovanni or the coda to the Leonore overture, with a specifically contrapuntal theme, points d'orgue, and a high C for the soprano all complete.
>
> What is more, the work which follows, entitled Night Falls On The Gods, is a thorough grand opera. In it you shall see what you have so far missed, the opera chorus in full parade on the stage, not presuming to interfere with the prima donna as she sings her death song over the footlights. Nay, that chorus will have its own chance when it first appears, with a good roaring strain in C major, not, after all, so very different from, or at all less absurd than the choruses of courtiers in La Favorita or "Per te immenso giubilo" in Lucia. The harmony is no doubt a little developed, Wagner augmenting his fifths with a G sharp where Donizetti would have put his fingers in his ears and screamed for G natural. But it is an opera chorus all the same; and along with it we have theatrical grandiosities that recall Meyerbeer and Verdi: pezzi d'insieme for all the principals in a row, vengeful conjurations for trios of them, romantic death song for the tenor: in short, all manner of operatic conventions.[7]

As a twenty-four-year-old novice composer in 1837, Wagner attended a performance of Bellini's *Norma* in Riga. He was overwhelmed. "It is not a crime to believe in this music," he remarked. "People think that I detest the entire Italian school, in particular Bellini. This is not true—a thousand times no! Bellini is my first preference because there is strength in his vocal writing and his music lends itself so perfectly to the original text." The long-term influence of the experience on the conclusion of the *Ring* and on the general musical-dramatic style of *Götterdämmerung* is palpable. The heroines of both opera commit suicide by immolation, of course. But this is only the most obvious similarity. In *Götterdämmerung*, music drama cedes to opera—to Italian opera in particular. Opera contains duets, ensembles, and choruses. Above all, opera foregrounds singing: the predominance and authority of the singing voice in general, and the female singing voice in particular. The Brünnhilde of *Die Walküre* and *Siegfried* speaks in music; this is the Wagnerian aesthetic. In act 2 of *Die Walküre* she listened to Wotan's twisted commands and was confused; she remained confused through the delivery of her ghastly punishment at the opera's end. In her short scene at the end of *Siegfried*, she exults at the arrival of the young hero, then rejects him in the name of her remembered godhood and virginity, and finally accepts him. Increasingly through the long course of *Götterdämmerung*, she sings, generating knowledge and wisdom, and the increasing reliability of both, through her voice.

Consider, for example, the oath scene in the Hall of the Gibichungs at the center of act 2. Siegfried defends himself against Brünnhilde's accusation of betrayal. He attempts inarticulately to assert his innocence, his verbal confusion exacerbated by a crisis of musical incompetence. Still amnesiac, he cannot participate in the ongoing musical vocabulary. He struggles and fails to get on top of the leitmotifs. By this point in the action, the listener is likely to be more literate in the recollection of leitmotifs than Siegfried. The listener can thus be expected to hear Siegfried's musical inadequacy, to hold him in some contempt despite his innocence. Indeed, the listener may be counted on to listen to Siegfried's efforts while silently correcting the notes he is singing. This involves a double correction. First, the leitmotifs need to be intoned correctly; secondly, they and their musical connective tissue need to be rendered with lyrical and harmonic viability. This is precisely what Brünnhilde does in response. Not knowing that Siegfried is ignorant of his own mendacity, Brünnhilde pushes him away from the spear he is swearing with, replaces his oath with her own, and contradicts him. Her music—"Helle Wehr! Heilige Waffe!" (Shining weapon! Hallowed blade!)—instantly claims the level of articulation and lyricism that eluded Siegfried. Brünnhilde easily controls the motivic language and achieves lyrical as well as personal authority by liberating herself from the burden of leitmotivic submission; she makes music, singing herself out of the musical, hegemonic structure of the *Ring* and its musical rhetoric. Paradoxically, Brünnhilde is deluded in words and action but lucid in music.

At this moment, having lost the ring from her hand, Brünnhilde takes control of the *Ring*, *qua* music drama, plot, and style. At the same time, she reinstates music drama (correcting Siegfried) and escapes it. Unlike Siegfried, she gets the musical and dramatic rhetoric right. But at the same moment, she uses that mastery to push aside the strictures of the system. Thus her position with regard to music drama recalls Walther von Stolzing's to the rules of the *Meisterlied*. In *Die Meistersinger von Nurnberg* (1868), this young singer is educated to respect musical laws in order to transcend them. At that opera's end, with an integrative conservatism consistent with its comic form, the young outsider is persuaded to become a complete insider and join the ranks of the mastersingers who once rejected him and whom he continues to disdain. Brünnhilde, like the tragic epic that surrounds her, never gains reintegration. Related to this eventuality, her externality, at the moment of her rebellion, to the aesthetic system that surrounds her—music drama—is more pronounced. Brünnhilde's rebelliousness gains stature and danger by adopting a style that is literally foreign to the form, namely the voice of Italian opera. Suddenly she is Norma. The authority of the gods and music drama broken, the world reverts to humanity and the human voice. For this reason, it is a necessary sacrilege to assert that *Götterdämmerung*, the telos and denouement of Wagner's *Ring*, may stand among the greatest of Italian operas.

The thesis has a problem, however, insofar as Brünnhilde's and music drama's discovery of an inner operatic unconscious bursts forth at a moment of misunderstanding rather than understanding. The center of *Götterdämmerung*'s act 2 endures: Brünnhilde's double accusation against Siegfried—his alleged guilt of both infidelity and perjury—is misguided and possible entirely unwarranted. The moral and legal case is complex and even opaque. Siegfried and Brünnhilde are virgin lovers at the conclusion of the opera that bears his name. Siegfried leaves Brünnhilde for some masculine adventure, which leads him down the Rhine to the Gibichungs and their entrapment of him. Dosed with a potion of forgetfulness, Siegfried forgets Brünnhilde and agrees to win her for Gunther. He does so, spending the night with Brünnhilde but swearing chastity both beforehand (to himself and the audience) and afterward (to the assembled Gibichungs and their courtiers). Functionally or intentionally, however, Wagner's drama does not clinch the case one way or the other. Brünnhilde's cave is ultimately related to the Marabar Caves of E. M. Forster's *A Passage to India*, to the dark and largely undiscovered interiors and their production of exaggerated echoes, which foreclose on both clarity and certainty. Forster's (anti-) heroine Adela Quested is somehow undone by her time inside the cave—as several of the novel's key British characters are undone by India itself—

prompting her to enter a charge of sexual assault against her Indian Muslim guide Dr. Aziz. Although the novel is sympathetic to Aziz, no clarification of what happened in the cave is forthcoming. Opaque to the novel's characters themselves, the caves and their secrets remain opaque to us readers as well. Similarly, though we reasonably assume Siegfried's innocence and his victimization at the hands of the Gibichungs, we do not have the evidence that would assure his abstemiousness with Brünnhilde on his return to her rock. The contortions of both the opera's plot and its textual legacy combine with the implied argument of sexual mystery to impede our control over facts and events. And we may reasonably wonder whether Brünnhilde's vindictive vehemence, her incapacity to think through a confusion of evidence, may point to a trauma of rape (as in some of the source texts) or else symptomatize some kind of sexual confusion not completely different from Forster's Miss Quested's. Brünnhilde emerges as a kind of anti-Isolde in the authenticity (emotional and musical) of her oath against her lover; Isolde, we know from the leitmotivic content of her curses, is repressing her love when she curses her unacknowledged object of desire. Brünnhilde's solo *cri de coeur* (*Ach Jammer! Jammer!*) followed by her participation in a fundamentally Italian vengeance trio together with Gunther and Hagen, adds up much more to a total release than a repression of conflicted emotion. Her eventual appraisal of the "truth" of Siegfried's innocence comes later (between the two scenes of act 3 of *Götterdämmerung*), through a reported encounter, which we also do not witness, with the three Rhinemaidens, who may or may not be reliable sources. Is there a chance that the operatic unconscious, its association with unmediated vocalization, with Nietzsche's southerly winds, may be a trap as well as a liberator, like too much exposure to the unconscious? Perhaps Thomas Mann had this possibility in mind when, Wagnerian that he was, he had his repressed northerly hero Gustav von Aschenbach of *Death in Venice* (1911) fall ill and die from a sickness carried—*contra* Nietzsche—by a toxic wind from the south.

FOUR

Les passions humaines

1. *Les passions humaines*

WHAT DO THE THREE NORNS KNOW, AND WHEN DO THEY know it? The knowledge possessed by the original Norns, singing in Bayreuth in 1876, would have included the genealogy of the great work in which they play a part: its origin in Wagner's wish to retell the story of Siegfried's death, and the ultimate realization of the tetralogy in the shadow of the academic discovery of the four-part structure of the *Oresteia* of Aeschylus. Later Norns would also know something, presumably, of the post-1876 history of Wagner staging: the Bayreuth realism that reigned until the Second World War; Wieland Wagner's modernist minimalism of the 1950s; Patrice Chéreau's radical historicism of 1976; and the many *Regieoper* efforts, from Wieland Wagner to Guy Cassiers. Finally the three Norns entering the conversation in March 2013 would likely know something about the style and argument of the production whose completion begins to unfold as their own narration takes shape. They would know, for example, that, from *Das Rheingold* onward, the stage has offered its spectators in Berlin and Milan a visual leitmotif in the form of a panoramic quotation of a hidden masterpiece: Jef Lambeaux's 1898 sculptural frieze known as *Les passions humaines*. They would *not* know that, at the end of the opera they unwittingly introduce, a three-dimensional, blazing white double of the frieze would descend into view at the front of the proscenium, fixing and ratifying the shared claim of Lambeaux's *Passions humaines* and the full *Ring* cycle as shared testimony to human reality, fallibility, and tragedy.

Audiences in Berlin and Milan who had been following Cassiers's *Ring* had been gazing on Lambeaux's frieze—or, more accurately, on multiple quotations of it—from the opening tableau of the second scene of *Das Rheingold*. Cassiers and his team—including the designer Enrico Bagnoli and the video artists Arjen Klerkx and Kurt D'Haeseleer—anchored the stage to a divisible fiberglass rendering of the Lambeaux frieze. The fiberglass's translucency enabled it to receive projections from both front and back. These projections combined visibly with the Lambeaux material. They could dominate completely, so that the Lambeaux itself would disappear from view; or, as in the conclusions of *Das Rheingold* and *Götterdämmerung*, they could themselves recede entirely in favor of the visual force of the full sculptural relief. In scene 2 of *Das Rheingold*, the frieze projected the panoramic worldview from Valhalla, a landscape that combined appealing mountain vistas with a distinct veneer of environmental and degradation, the latter emerging, as mentioned earlier, through fleeting references to the problems of strip mining and landscape degradation in the manner of the photographer Edward Burtynsky. Serving, at *Rheingold*'s conclusion, as the portal into the gods' new castle itself, the frieze revealed its own images in their full dimensionality, but colored now a deep and somehow disturbing golden hue, as if to embody the greed and excess of the occupying gods. In *Die Walküre* and *Siegfried*, the Lambeaux frieze reappeared both in vertical fragments and in its entirety. It revealed the battle montage—reminiscent of the television coverage of the 1990 Gulf War—that opened act 2 of *Die Walküre*. The young Siegfried forged his sword to images of firebombing and ruined cityscapes, suggesting the destructive potential of the power that the naive hero reconstitutes so naively. Siegfried's exposure to this violent potential appears limited to a few video screens—the perspective of the protected adolescent, and not unlike Alberich's highly mediatized power perch in scene 3 of *Das Rheingold*. Siegfried's conquest of Brünnhilde was set against a severe gray-and-white articulation of the frieze, a portent of its overwhelming final appearance at the conclusion of *Götterdämmerung*. Here, in a gesture of doubling and repetition, we the audience seem to be warned that the debacle we have witnessed will be repeated in our own time and lives, and therefore with increased immediacy to our fields of vision and experience. We remain inside this story.

Each appearance of the Lambeaux frieze on Cassiers's stage is thus highly textured, both literally and metaphorically, both visually and dramaturgically. This visual and dramatic multiplicity renders these images quite precisely as visual analogs to the musical texture of Wagner's score in general and to the function of the musical leitmotifs in particular. The production's visual leitmotifs, like Wagner's musical ones, are repetitive and somehow recognizable, but their repetitions are always destabilized by difference, so that the sense of recognition never delivers a constant object of recognition. The leitmotif—musical and visual—thus emerges as an *act of referring* rather than as a reference to a fixed object or idea. That act of referring is contingent on its moment, and it refers also to prior as well as subsequent instances of the leitmotif through the course of the tetralogy. Leitmotifs, musical and visual, are built from both basic and conflicting elements in Wagner's musical dramatic practice: namely, action and narration.

The *Götterdämmerung* story and text mark the place where Wagner first sketched the plan of the *Ring* as the story of Siegfried's death. The increasing need and heft of the backstory required to account for Siegfried's story produced the three preceding works, which Wagner then composed in forward order. As the tetralogy's text evolved, he still wished to maintain the priority of the denouement. The original idea of the action-opera supported by a long, indeed ever lengthening set-up continued to dominate the explicit aesthetic—musical and dramatic—of the entire final tetralogy. This aesthetic gives stated priority to action over narration. Yet the *Ring's* evolution displays a persistent overtaking of structure by scaffold, of story by backstory, of action by narration. *Das Rheingold*, *Die Walküre*, and *Siegfried* are as important as *Götterdämmerung*. And the cycle's narrations, from Loge's in *Das Rheingold* to Brünnhilde's at the end of *Götterdämmerung*, equal and perhaps overtake the action scenes for their depth and subtlety of musical form and portrayed human complexity.

In this evolving structure, the musical leitmotif becomes the nucleus, the microcosm of the action-narration dyad. The leitmotif becomes the hybrid, as counterintuitive as this may be, of action and narration. Every leitmotif resounds as an event in the present moment—just as every musical utterance (in a live performance) is played by a musician and his or her instrument at the moment of its hearing. Nevertheless, with the exquisite exceptions of those instances at the start of *Das Rheingold* where these utterances are played and heard for the first time, these phrases regularly refer to past articulations, to the existential gap between past and present, and to the memory or forgetting of the past from the standpoint of the present. If, for example, we sense on first hearing that the glorious sounds and mood of the chords signaling Brünnhilde's awakening in the final scene of *Siegfried* will not assure the lovers' happy future, the uncannily melancholy sound and feel of their repetition at the opening of *Götterdämmerung* redefine them retroactively as harbingers more of doom than of joy. This overtaking of joy by doom is finally sealed by the same music's accompaniment of Siegfried's death. The "repetition with difference" is poignant, suggesting that the youthful awakening of eros is matched by the knowledge that accrues in anticipation of death. Doom is thus imprinted on joy, death on life, tragedy on comedy.

Imprinting is a visual metaphor more than a musical one, of course. It speaks, therefore, more literally to the function of Lambeaux's *Passions humaines* as a series of visual leitmotifs. As we begin to recognize, visually, the relief and its fragments through the imprints of the fiberglass reproduction and its overlays of projected images, we build a vocabulary of meaningful and interrelated images, a visual score analogous to the musical score that Wagner provides. Its simultaneous visual and spatial overlays, moreover, become analogous to the musical and temporal overlays of the score and its invocations of leitmotifs.

Wagner began textually with *Götterdämmerung* and ends there musically. By the time he arrives there musically and dramatically, however, the very architecture with which he has built the *Ring* has begun to destabilize. More of an opera than a music drama, *Götterdämmerung* in its riveting passion and momentum seems always to live in the *now*, at the moment now unfolding onstage. The disappearance from the story of Wotan has removed the *longue durée* of the gods from the story, as does the breaking of the Norns' narrative rope in the prologue. Waltraute's visit to Brünnhilde seems like one from a different planet, let alone a different social realm.

Götterdämmerung is a story of human passions. There are no gods here. If Brünnhilde has a godly provenance, she is entirely human here. Her transformation is both a reduction and an ennoblement. Though Siegfried encountered and battled a god in his quick victory over Wotan, his unhappy childhood and ruined adulthood mark him as completely and sadly human. The telos of an epic of the gods is a fully human story, and also a story of descent into the human realm.

Their human profiles notwithstanding, Siegfried's journey from Brünnhilde's rock to the world of the Gibichungs and his subsequent abduction and delivery of Brünnhilde to the same miserable destination form a variation on the standard mythical trope of the gods' descent into the human world. In the basic version of this global myth—so prevalent in the Olympian system and in later Christianized stories, among many others— the god descends to the human world to find exceptional goodness among a norm of selfishness, and through that goodness a way to godly as well as human redemption. For example, Ovid, in one of the founding myths of hospitality, relates (in *Metamorphoses* VIII) the story of the elderly peasant couple Philemon and Baucis, who extend their modest household to two peasant visitors who turn out to be Zeus and Hermes in disguise. Inheriting this paradigm, the operatic canon is full of stories of "high" couples gaining wisdom and ethical grounding from "low" ones: think of Tamino and Pamina in Mozart's *The Magic Flute* and, much more explicitly, their twentieth-century descendants, the Emperor and Empress in Richard Strauss and Hugo von Hofmannsthal's *Die Frau ohne Schatten*.

Other mythologies offer variations on this parable of descent. In a significant Hindu variant, gods who have transgressed in some way in heaven are punished with a sentence of descent to a sordid earth and mortality. Their reward, ultimately, is to be killed and thereby recalled to heavenly life. This is not unlike the myth of Valhalla as announced by Brünnhilde in act 2 of *Die Walküre*. Brünnhilde simply assumes that Siegmund will agree to human death in order to follow her to Valhalla.

Here in *Götterdämmerung*, however, the code is different. Brünnhilde and Siegfried, two essentially benevolent creatures, involved with and possibly doomed by their traffic with the gods, find treachery and evil in the world of the humans, and are ruined by the toxic webs of humanity. There is no Valhalla to return to, as Valhalla has itself been fatally compromised by its intercourse with the lower worlds. Why is this human world so degraded?

Musically, Wagner introduces us to the world of Hagen and the Gibichungs twice. The first and more celebrated introduction, bridging the opera's prologue and first act, is known as Siegfried's Rhine Journey. Opening with Siegfried's horn call, a quote from the orchestra of the sound of the young hero's greeting to the world, this orchestral fantasy quickly gathers power and momentum to amount in a short time to a musical biography of a young hero with a big future. It's the first tone poem, the prototype of Strauss's *Ein Heldenleben* and *Till Eulenspiegels lustige Streiche*. Within the unfolding of *Götterdämmerung*, it becomes, proleptically, the proposition that will be answered finally by Siegfried's own funeral music, which will renarrate the same biography as a broken dream. This is a big story, bigger than suggested by the amount of time it fills, as if the orchestra were instructing the young Siegfried (to reverse the famous words of Gurnemanz to Parsifal): "Zur Zeit wird hier das Raum" (Here space becomes time). The spirited and optimistic Rhine Journey ends with a dark cadence as it delivers us, the audience, slightly in advance of Siegfried himself, to the Hall of the Gibichungs. Here lodge Siegfried's future and fate, and in some way Germany and Europe's post-1876 future as well. This post-1876 future, unknown to Wagner, is part of the cultural memory of later generations of audiences.

The second musical introduction to the world of the Gibichungs is the extraordinary act 2 prelude and the dark, brooding melody to which Hagen will proclaim to Alberich the maternal inheritance of his own misery:

> Gab mir die Mutter Mut,
> nicht mag ich ihr doch danken,
> dass deiner List sie erlag:
> frühalt, fahl und bleich,
> hass' ich die Frohen,
> freue mich nie!

> Though my mother gave me courage
> I am not inclined to thank her
> For subjecting me to your cunning:
> Prematurely old, sickly, and pale,
> I hate the happy ones,
> take pleasure in nothing.

In disposition, Hagen is the opposite of Siegfried, who tried in the forest to imagine the beauty of his dead mother. Politically, just as much as vocally, Hagen is the heir of Fafner, hoarding not gold but a legacy of frustration and rage. Hagen, Fafner, and Hunding share the same stentorian bass voice and often, and to excellent effect, the same singer. The stunning music both of the act 2 prelude and the short, devastating scene between Hagen and his father—a sequence that Wagner claimed to work harder on than on any other—captures the dark side of the European "world of our fathers": the side which, "taking possession of an accursed inheritance," as Joseph Conrad wrote in *Heart of Darkness*, will result in misery, evil, and violence, to be "subdued at the cost of profound anguish and of excessive toil." If the second act of *Siegfried* offered a parable of the descent into the unconscious, the world of Hagen and the Gibichungs pulls us, as Conrad does, into a heart of darkness that is political and historical as much as psychological and moral.

We can invoke Conrad here in the shadow of the earlier discussion (chapter 1) of the Belgian political context of Lambeaux's *Passions humaines*. Conrad's 1899 novella shadowed the author's own journey, undertaken in 1890-91 to the Belgian Congo in the employ of the Société Anonyme du Haut-Congo and his service as captain of the Congo River steamship *Roi des Belges*. The ship was named for Belgian's King Leopold II, who, with the help of the British explorer H. M. Stanley, had claimed and built a colonial empire in the Congo that generated a global trade in ivory and rubber, enabled by the literal enslavement and general violent abuse of the indigenous population. Conrad's exposure of that system follows his narrator, Marlow, on an expedition named "Eldorado" (The Golden) up the Congo River to the supply station managed by Mr. Kurtz:

> Going up that river was like travelling back to the earliest beginnings of the world, when vegetation rioted on the earth and the big trees were kings.... you lost your way on that river as you would in a desert, and butted all day long against shoals, trying to find the channel, till you thought yourself bewitched and cut off for ever from everything you had known once—somewhere—far away—in another existence perhaps. There were moments when one's past came back to one, as it will sometimes when you have not a moment to spare to yourself; but it came in the shape of an unrestful and noisy dream, remembered with wonder amongst the overwhelming realities of this strange world of plants, and water, and silence. And this stillness of life did not in the least resemble a peace.

Conrad knew Wagner's works and, in a remarkable coincidence recounted by his friend and collaborator Ford Madox Ford, once weathered a fierce storm from the fourth floor of a Belgian coastal hotel to the sounds of a stentorian contralto practicing music from *Götterdämmerung* in the basement.[1] The link is more profound than that, however.

Though Wagner's Hagen predates Conrad's Kurtz by almost a quarter of a century, we have every reason to imagine Hagen as a precursor or analog to the colonial stationmaster who has become the icon of the colonial system, of its psychic and political corruption and its "institutional extremism." This last phrase is the coinage of the historian Isabel Hull with regard to the German genocide of the Herero in German South West Africa (modern Namibia) between 1904 and 1907, a process that Hull describes as the passage from suppression to annihilation.[2] Hagen, the son of Alberich, and the Gibichungs thus take on the guise of the low-level master of the enslaved, answering to the adventures of metropolitan authority. This is the context that pays homage to the haunting gravitas of Hagen's Watch at the conclusion of act 1, scene 1, as well as his mocking arousal of the Gibichungs in the scene that follows. It is a context that clarifies as well the stakes and extent of the destruction and self-destruction brought about by Siegfried's collaboration with Hagen and Gunther, in other words by the collaboration of the elites with the slavemasters.

> Hier sitz' ich zur Wacht,
> wahre den Hof,
> wehre die Halle dem Feind.
> ....
> Ihr freien Söhne,
> frohe Gesellen,
> segelt nur lustig dahin!
> Dünkt er euch niedrig,
> ihr dient ihm doch,
> des Niblungen Sohn.

> Here I sit and watch,
> protecting the castle,
> arming the hall against the enemy.
> ....
> You free sons,
> cheerful youths,
> sail happily forth!
> Though you think him base,
> in fact you serve him,
> the Nibelung's son.

It was in 1897 or 1898, writes Adam Hochschild at the opening of *King Leopold's Ghost*, his celebrated history of the Belgian occupation of the Congo and the abolitionists who helped end it, that full knowledge of the colonial system's violence began to reach European readers. That news arrived thanks in part to the work of a shipping company employee turned journalist and activist named Edward Morel on his return from the Congo River Basin to the home port of Antwerp.[3] It is thus more than probable that the Antwerp-born sculptor Jef Lambeaux knew of these realities when he cast his giant frieze *Les passions humaines* in 1898. In this context, the violence of *Les passions humaines* takes on a specific historical reference to the enslavement of Africa that accompanied the global modernization of the nineteenth century. The censorship of that content, as carried out by every ruler from the king of Belgium to the kings of Saudi Arabia, forms a dimension of that same global history. The appearance and fundamental importance of the Lambeaux frieze on Cassiers's Wagner stage affirms the power of this production as a completely original and deeply responsible dialogue with the complex world and afterlife of Richard Wagner.

Siegfried's journey takes him down the Rhine. That is clear. As powerful a metaphor as it is a location, the Rhine signifies the source and center of the German world, a journey down it the passage from center to periphery. Wagner's literal geography is intra-German. Nevertheless, as the declaration of the German Second Empire in 1871 gives way to the belated imperialism of the 1880s (marked most theatrically by the 1884 Conference on Africa, known also as the Congo Conference, which took place on Berlin's Wilhelmstrasse), the German journey to the periphery acquired a global claim and reach. Siegfried's journey to a realm of incomprehensibility, forgetfulness, and uncanny evil resonates with the journey up Conrad's river; Hagen's realm has something to do with Kurtz's. That Hagen is the son of Alberich, and thus a member of the original family of the *Ring*'s plot, only reinforces the duality of familiarity and exoticism: the structure of the uncanny (the *unheimlich*) as the fusion of the familiar and the defamiliarized, the homely and the unhomely.

For the Hall of the Gibichungs, Cassiers and his team reached out to a fairly standard Hollywood trope of the uncanny, but with startling visual results. The space's partitions, walls, and occasional mobile furniture all consisted of cabinets of curiosities, filled with human limbs and other body parts floating in clear space or, perhaps, liquid (fig. 4.1). The edges of civilization—or, more accurately, occupation—conjure mad science and brutal torture. The association with Lambeaux's *Passions humaines* is palpable here. Even more so is the evocation of the severed hands of King Leopold's African victims. At the start of act 1, scene 2, Gunther and Gutrune roll into view seated on a low version of the grotesque cabinet; creatures imported from Luchino Visconti's (and Klaus Mann's) *The Damned*, they appear sipping a digestif from crystal glasses set on a silver tray. The choruses of the Gibichung men and women will also arrive and recede atop such cabinets (now forming steps or bleachers); they are also complicit players in the Gibichungs' uncanny regime. Finally, Siegfried's corpse will be rolled in on the same structure that delivered Gutrune and Gunther, and Brünnhilde will make her way through a still higher bleacher toward her Immolation Scene (fig. 4.2).

FIG. 4.1. *Götterdämmerung*, acts 2 and 3: Gibichungs' curiosity cabinets. Photo: Michael P. Steinberg.

2. Awakenings

Perhaps my single most exciting second as a young operagoer (and I do mean literally the measure of a second, neither a sixty-second minute nor an abstract moment) took place on March 8, 1974, during the prologue of *Götterdämmerung* at the Metropolitan Opera. This was the production's premiere, the final installment of the long-delayed and derailed *Ring* that Herbert von Karajan had abandoned, both as conductor and director, following *Die Walküre*. Rafael Kubelik was conducting as part of his short-lived assignment as the company's music director, and Birgit Nilsson was scheduled to sing Brünnhilde. Three days earlier the *New York Times* had reported that Nilsson had sustained a fall during a dress rehearsal and broken several ribs. She was therefore not expected to sing the long and challenging role in the early performances. Rumors circulated about a possible replacement but named no one.

Still a high school student, I had snagged a ticket to the premiere through the ever miraculous and generous connection of my high school to the Metropolitan Opera Guild. Having spent a good deal of my free time

FIG. 4.2. *Götterdämmerung*, act 3: Brünnhilde's immolation. Photo: Koen Broos.

during my high school years at the Met, both as a spectator and also as a supernumerary, I knew the majority of the house staff, including the ushers, and many of them also knew me, having evicted me more than once out of orchestra and box seats in which I did not belong. One of the strictest of the ushers was "Bob," most likely the *nom d'opéra* attached to this portly, aristocratic octogenarian of distinctly Teutonic origin. On that Friday afternoon, March 8, I happened to meet Bob on the street as I walked home from school. "Who will sing Brünnhilde tonight?" I asked him, as no announcement had been made. "Is there any chance Nilsson will sing?" "I sink she vill sing," he prophesied.

A committed teenage opera fan at the time, I was also a confessed Nilsson groupie. I had delivered a three-dollar bouquet of roses to the Met's stage door (purchased from a street vendor on Broadway) when she sang Isolde in November 1971. I also held a slight grudge against her, as my third supernumerary role at the Met (following my Philistine soldier in *Samson et Dalila* and my Egyptian soldier in *Aida*) was to be a sailor in *Tristan* (act 1) until, I was told, Nilsson had requested a less saturated stage. No matter: in the 1970s Nilsson owned the Wagner and Strauss *Heldensopran* roles, and her *Götterdämmerung* Brünnhilde was going to add up either to a great event or to a tragic absence.

Much to my surprise, leaning over the fifth-tier, family-circle (side) balcony, no ominous yellow spotlight appeared on the pre-performance curtain, the light that always signaled a cast substitution and always summoned a groan from the 3,800 members of the Met audience. Kubelik entered the pit and conducted the Norn scene. The feeling of electricity in the house intensified palpably as the dawn music announced the scene change to Brünnhilde's rock. The lights flashed on, and as the orchestra delivered the *Götterdämmerung* love motif, Nilsson emerged smiling from the set's cave, one arm in a sling, with Siegfried (Jess Thomas) just behind her, smiling more in recognition of a diva than of his new lover. I don't think anyone thought of the pair as Siegfried and Brünnhilde at that moment. This was raw opera. Here was Thomas smiling back at Nilsson in the awed anticipation that she would now, with several broken ribs, embark on this performance. At that moment, the Met audience jumped from our seats and roared. This was no articulated "brava" or anything beyond the most visceral shout of joy from close to four thousand people. It lasted only a beat; Kubelik had no need to pause and wisely chose not to, thereby increasing the voltage of the moment and of the evening as a whole. Nilsson's entrance produced an operatic and human thrill; it had nothing to do with Wagner

FIG. 4.3. *Götterdämmerung*, prologue: Norns. Photo: Koen Broos.

or with *Götterdämmerung*. Nevertheless, the musical and emotional excitement of the Brünnhilde-Siegfried scene is well served by this kind of thrill and energy. I can't think of a performance of the scene, since 1974, that has ridden a similar wave.

Cassiers's direction of *Götterdämmerung*'s opening sequence found a different kind of momentum, lower key but also grounded in a sustainable dramatic argument. In the staging for Berlin and Milan, the three Norns delivered their scene perched on a version of Brünnhilde's rock, now covered in sheets of fabric that bore a distant relation to the bright red cords that carried their narration (fig. 4.3).

From the death of Fasolt in scene 4 of *Das Rheingold*, descending red lines had marked places and instances of death on the stage, multiplying exponentially for the Ride of the Valkyries. The visual leitmotif now communicated a new pathos as the Norns' narration assumed a visual correlative defined by death. At the conclusion of their scene, the three Norns slowly descended upstage from the rock, dragging the fabric cover along with them. The bared rock, a Rubik's cube of ragged squares, revealed now a figure sleeping on top of it. As the figure became discernible as the Siegfried, Brünnhilde entered from the negative space at upstage left, climbing the rock from behind to awaken Siegfried with a kiss. The symmetry here was clear: Brünnhilde's awakening of Siegfried with a kiss supplied the precise inversion of the awakening of Brünnhilde in the final scene of *Siegfried*. The gesture's sustainability consisted in its marking the remainder of the long night of *Götterdämmerung* as the story of Siegfried's awakening.

The singers did not like the rock. It was in fact somewhat dangerous, especially when its fabric cover or the excessively long trains of the women's costumes snagged one of its treacherous corners. But it had occasional rewards. In the scene between Brünnhilde and Waltraute, the visit between two sisters which begins warmly but ends badly, two of its concave spaces unexpectedly formed the equivalent of two chairs and a table. The two sisters were poised as if sharing tea in a thoroughly Victorian setting, with all its suggestions of the intimacy that masks contempt—another version of the alliance between the *heimlich* and *unheimlich*.

The *Ring*, recall, offers numerous awakening scenes. Each one casts a unique cognitive and emotional significance not only on the state of awakening, but also on the state of sleep that precedes the awakening. Erda's sleep, presumably at all times but explicitly so on her unwelcome awakening via Wotan's harsh calls in act 3 of *Siegfried*, is the sleep of wisdom: she is awakened here "aus wissendem Schlaf." Fafner's sleep, in act 2 of *Siegfried*, is the sleep of ignorance. Brünnhilde's twenty-year sleep between *Walküre* and *Siegfried* hovers indeterminately between these two extremes. Siegfried's sleep (one night's? many nights'?) with Brünnhilde is not flagged at all by Wagner, beyond his opening remark about how much he has learned from his lover. She has apparently conferred on him the capacity for knowledge; his inhabitation of that knowledge, his awakening to consciousness of the world, will accrue late—too late—across the action of *Götterdämmerung*.

Cassiers's innovative staging marks this point of the opera as Siegfried's awakening. There are two additional options available to the central metaphor of awakening. First and most conventionally is the second awakening of Brünnhilde, not this time from sleep but from delusion, the delusion of Siegfried's betrayal as staged by Hagen. She is informed, too late, of the truth by the Rhinemaidens, a scene that Wagner interestingly chooses not to represent—a sure sign of his own persuasion, late in the game, of the authority of narration over action. The result is her declaration of total knowledge at the moment not only of her death but that of the gods and their world: "Alles weiss ich; alles ward mir nun klar" (I know everything; everything has become clear to me). The third option deanthromorphizes and therefore cannot be staged through human characters, and that is the Hegelian option of knowledge as its own subject: the birth of knowledge that knows. Conceivably, Wagner had such an abstraction in mind when he gave the authoritative ending of the *Ring* not to Brünnhilde, as originally planned, but to the orchestra. In this guise, unpersonified knowledge in the *Ring* becomes analogous to the unpersonified and unobjectified desire in Mozart and Da Ponte's *Così fan tutte*, whose ending also cannot be staged via the resolutions and fates of its characters.

The postcoital morning we witness in the *Götterdämmerung* prologue involves the exchange of gifts: Brünnhilde gives Siegfried her horse, Grane, in exchange for the Ring, now redefined from a dormant agent of power into a token of love. Siegfried remains ignorant of the Ring's power, while Brünnhilde apparently does not think twice about sending Siegfried off without this ultimate weapon. Yet this transfer of gifts contains another and far more interesting implication. At this moment in the drama Brünnhilde, electing to remain on her rock, cedes the opera's action to Siegfried, who will take not only the action but also the orchestra with him as he cruises down the Rhine into the nasty hands of Hagen and the Gibichungs, toward a recapitulation of the hostile hospitality that Hunding offered Siegmund, his father. What the current production strove quite innovatively to imply is that Brünnhilde is also ceding to Siegfried the capacity for knowledge, in other words ceding to him both the hope of conscious knowledge and the burdens of the unconscious. In one of music drama's proto-psychoanalytic insights, the capacity for knowledge is understood here as the companion of the unconscious. To push the hypothesis one step further: Brünnhilde transfers her own unconscious to Siegfried. Brünnhilde channels Norma, as Siegfried channels Tristan. Let me try to enlarge and defend this pair of claims, which may appear excessive on first impression, at the same time taking responsibility for them as possibilities opened by Cassiers's stage but certainly not argued explicitly.

Bellini's *Norma* impressed Wagner profoundly in 1839, as we have seen. Norma's final self-immolation together with her treacherous but remorseful lover, Pollione, sets a solid precedent for the denouement of *Götterdämmerung*. In this light, Nietzsche may have made an empirical error when he skewered Wagner for importing a version of the Hindu ritual of suttee into his music drama. The analogy may be apt (and indeed all the more tempting in the shadow of the German scholarship of classical India that emerged during the three decades between Wagner's story and Nietzsche's critique), but the direct influence may be off the mark.[4] Moreover, my own claim that the vocal and dramatic thrust of act 2 of *Götterdämmerung* lifts its style and action out of the bed of music drama and into that of Italian opera adds ballast to *Norma* and its style as a significant precedent. The question remains of how deep the resonance remains and what precisely counts as its components.

Bellini's orchestra and Norma's coloratura style remain out of the picture here, to be sure. Something deeper seems to be at stake. There is a certain lack in the drama and texture of the Italian tradition that runs, I will risk asserting, throughout the grand tradition from Bellini through Verdi and even Puccini. This lack may in fact run through Italian discursive, literary, and aesthetic representations in general. This is the lack of a discursive dimension addressing the unconscious. The implication here, to be clear, is decidedly not that Italians have no unconscious. Such a claim would be not only outright silly but would also contradict the basic tenet of the universality of the human unconscious. It would therefore undermine the very deployment of the category. The point is rather that representational practices do not feel the need to make themselves vulnerable to the rifts and pressures that the unconscious imposes on consciousness and representations, a need that in my view comes from the recognition of fundamental cultural differences and rifts as basic to human experience and everyday life. That the systematic recognition and, second, theorization of the unconscious came from the German (or, more precisely, the German-speaking) world connects to the foundational anxieties of that world produced by surviving elements (*Nachträglichkeit*, to use Freud's term) of the deepest religious and cultural divisions that mark and split Germany but not Italy. These divisions are not empirically relevant in Italy, or in France, for that matter, though their relative absence cannot be understood to free these national or proto-national entities from severe internal conflicts, defined differently. The German world needed the unconscious to understand itself collectively as well as individually.

Brünnhilde-as-Norma means Brünnhilde without her unconscious. This is the most basic and most devastating element of the psychic and stylistic transformation in control of both Brünnhilde and her opera in and beyond the grand operatic scene in the Hall of the Gibichungs in act 2. It determines the remainder of act 2 stylistically and dramatically, culminating in the great and positively Verdian revenge trio of Brünnhilde, Hagen, and Gunther. Offstage, it controls Brünnhilde until her belated briefing by the Rhinemaidens—which, as mentioned above, Wagner interestingly chooses not to show us—informing her that Siegfried's betrayal was the result of a trick. Her return to the stage to take up her assignment literally to stage the ending of the opera is marked first by the psychic weight of her restored unconscious, leading her to utter several opaque and strangely motivated remarks ("Kinder hört' ich greinen nach der Mutter, da süsser Milch sie verschüttet" [I heard children lamenting to their mother that she had spilled sweet milk]) before regaining her ultimate lucidity and purpose.

"Mehr gabst du, Wunderfrau, als ich zu wahren weiss" (Wondrous woman, you have given me more than I know how to sustain): Siegfried's opening salvo to Brünnhilde in the prologue may apply itself too glibly to the argument I am pursuing here. Nevertheless, it seems a worthy trial to suggest that the gift he obliquely and—by definition—unknowingly refers to is the gift of the unconscious, of Brünnhilde's own unconscious. When he departs on his Rhine Journey, Siegfried brings with him a state of anticipation and potential. The potential he carries, which will remain unrealized and unrecognized—by others, by the audience, and by himself—until the moment of his death, is that of an enriched psyche, one at once enabled and burdened by love. The precedent here is, clearly, Tristan.

The *Götterdämmerung* Siegfried for the Berlin premiere in March 2013 was Ian Storey, the British tenor who had risen to prominence as the Tristan in Patrice Chéreau and Daniel Barenboim's production for La Scala late in 2007. Storey's Tristan had evolved into a deeply considered dramatic portrayal. (I saw three of his performances: in Milan in January 2008 and February 2009, and in Berlin in March 2012). The performance was grounded first in a high degree of physical self-exposure and disclosure. Storey wore little make-up and no wig. His closely cropped gray hair counted especially as a signal of the characterization's low-key sincerity and maturity. Dramatically and emotionally, Storey's Tristan was centered in the look in his eyes—an aspect that was somewhat dissipated, to be sure, in the La Scala house but quite evident in the Schillertheater, as on the DVD from La Scala. That look was searing, melancholic, and inquisitive, inserting the character into a quandary of knowing, unknowing, and questioning rather than into a state of being. Of course this disposition became especially clear and articulated during the course of the wounded Tristan's delirious psychic excursions of act 3. But the very capacity of those excursions and their psychic depth and meaning had been motivated throughout, coached, presumably, by Chéreau and sustaining amply the generally accepted assumption that Tristan and Isolde's love potion serves as a placebo for the liberation of repressed torrents of love and attraction.

It was clear, during the weeks of rehearsal in February 2013, that Storey had brought much of his Tristan into the *Götterdämmerung* Siegfried. It became equally clear that this overlay could inscribe Storey's Siegfried with an unusual depth of character, carefully paced through the evening's long journey of learning and obfuscation, *Bildung* and anti-*Bildung*. My own conversations with Storey on these issues, some in the company of Cassiers and some not, became the most focused and most rewarding encounters over the course of my participation in the rehearsal period generally. They were complemented by conversations with Waltraud Meier, Storey's Isolde at La Scala and now Sieglinde and the Second Norn and Waltraute in *Götterdämmerung*. The more experienced Wagnerian, Meier had clearly coached Storey during the course of their stage partnership, and she now observed that his inhabitation of a certain melancholy disposition—from Tristan to Siegfried—had clearly honed his performance. Storey's work reclaimed this opera as Siegfried's story, focusing dramatic attention on what Siegfried knows and what his knowledge means to him. If Tristan's potion liberates his unconscious against the grasp of the previously intact authority of society, hierarchy, and law (all gathered under the general metaphor of the "day" as against the erotic and subversive realm of the "night"), Siegfried's potion does the opposite: it blocks his erotically constituted unconscious—his attachment to Brünnhilde—in favor of a debut in respectable society that includes a marriage (to Gutrune) of convenience, networking, and advancement. In both cases, however, the question of the unmasterable unconscious abides: Tristan's unconscious prior to the potion, Siegfried's after it—or, rather, during the course of its effect. What does Siegfried know and remember through his period of non-knowing and non-memory?

An early conversation with Storey addressed a banal but not insignificant circumstance of operatic contingency. If Hagen's potion causes Siegfried to forget his conquest of Brünnhilde, what does he still remember of his life prior to that event? What does the *Götterdämmerung* Siegfried recall of the *Siegfried* Siegfried? Storey hadn't in fact sung the *Siegfried* Siegfried and therefore didn't know the details of Cassiers's production. He didn't know (and was keen to learn) that Siegfried's first hint of erotic experience came from the Forest Bird, whose sounds were eroticized by way of the audience's vision of a beautiful female figure onstage, though she was invisible to Siegfried. This memory of a pre-Brünnhilde erotic inflection and awakening of erotic capacity would remain in Siegfried's memory as it would in the memory of the audience, however subliminally in both cases. Siegfried's surviving conscious memory of the forest bird would potentially preserve his memory of an erotic inclination, thus compromising at least slightly his memory block with regard to Brünnhilde. This residual conscious memory argues for at least a red thread into the memory of Brünnhilde, now repressed not into nonexistence but into Siegfried's unconscious. Both dimensions of memory would conceivably serve to render Siegfried's actions and comportment throughout act 2 and in act 3, scene 1 vulnerable to a degree of self-doubt and anxiety.

Siegfried's post-potion comportment in act 2 bears a limited but not uninteresting similarity to Tristan's pre-potion stance in act 1 of his opera. Tristan's honor-bound stiffness stifles, we assume even prior to the ample corroboration, a strong attraction to Isolde, the Irish princess whom he is ferrying to Cornwall to become the wife of King Marke. We learn from Isolde that an erotically charged moment had already passed between them, when the wounded Tristan had mesmerized her. When she then curses and claims to want to exorcise that erotic charge, her "curse music" takes the form of the slightest rhythmic and harmonic variation of the love motif that opened the opera's prelude and announced its basic content. (In this case we can in fact sidestep the question of the signifying capacity and function of the leitmotif, as the Tristan love motif is mimetic in its inscription of a surge of longing and desire.) The unconscious bond with Isolde that Tristan suppresses pre-potion is thus similar to the bond with Brünnhilde that Siegfried carries, post-potion, in his unconscious, rising to the surface through symptoms whose presence and expression depend on the discretion of the director and the singer.

Siegfried insists too much on his innocence and attraction to Gutrune. The "bad music" of his oath (see the previous chapter) argues for the repressed character of the sincerity and musicality that reside in his unconscious. This behavior continues in the odd scene with the Rhinemaidens in act 3. Following the initial lament of the Rhinemaidens about the lost gold, Siegfried appears, uttering the strange information that "ein Albe führte mich irr" (an elf has led me astray). This is a strange and opaque piece of information, unusually so in Wagner's textual economy, and possibly a sign that Wagner, like Siegfried, is symptomatizing here, as Siegfried returns, his motive unclear, to the scene of a crime. Not his crime, of course, but rather Alberich's, as we were recently been reminded by Waltraute in the final scene of act 1. Brünnhilde had refused to engage with her troubled sister on this issue, and somehow Siegfried now channels Brünnhilde's disavowal. When the Rhinemaidens ask him to return the Ring from his finger (echoing Waltraute's earlier request to Brünnhilde), he refuses, suggesting that he cannot waste on them what his wife has a legitimate claim on (his loyalty as well as the Ring). What he unknowingly reveals to us, the audience, is that, having forced the Ring from Brünnhilde's hand with a violence that may or may not be a metonym for an actual rape, he has not offered the Ring to Gutrune as he had done previously to Brünnhilde. A shallower devotion has apparently been in play in this alliance. It is also unclear what kind of wedding night Siegfried and Gutrune have by now enjoyed (or not). If the marriage has been consummated, then Siegfried has now betrayed Brünnhilde sexually. If the marriage was not consummated, if in fact Gutrune's agitation in the scene that will follow will be at least partially determined by sexual dissatisfaction, then it is also possible that residual, unconscious loyalty to Brünnhilde will have effected some sexual dysfunction on the night prior to Siegfried's strange walk in the forest. All of this we discussed with Storey, recommending that he place some of these unresolved issues into Siegfried's disposition at this point in the drama. Now changing their tone to one of authoritative reprimand, the Rhinemaidens' musical texture and momentum gain significant harmonic and rhythmic ballast. They cite the Norns' weaving of the narrative rope in the past tense, apparently aware that the rope has been broken; nevertheless they quote Brünnhilde's love music in prophesying that "ein stolzes Weib wird noch heute dich Argen beerben" (a proud woman [i.e., Brünnhilde herself] will inherit the Ring on this very day).

Siegfried thus carries real psychic baggage into act 3, scene 2 with Hagen, Gunther, and the Gibichung huntsmen. The initial banter among Siegfried, Hagen, and Gunther contains enough ominous signals for even the slowest wit to decipher, though Wagner's text and directions do not make this clear. For the moment when Siegfried finally pours onto the ground the drink that Gunther refused to imbibe, Cassiers asked Storey to make the gesture more portentous than nonchalant. The pouring of symbolic blood onto the earth thus became a small but sharp reminder of the thread of environmental degradation that had been running through the production. When Siegfried begins to narrate his life story to the men, he begins with his childhood, a part of his life unaffected by Hagen's potion. That narration, combined with the baggage evident earlier on, may grease the wheels of his memory of Brünnhilde just as much as the antidote that Hagen eventually administers.

The return of Siegfried's memory of Brünnhilde is the first of the three overwhelming denouements of the opera, to be followed by his funeral music and Brünnhilde's immolation. Siegfried's recovery of his memory must be cataclysmic, to him and to the audience. It becomes his charge to put virtually all of Tristan in act 3 into a few minutes of words and music. It is the moment when Siegfried takes hold of the same total knowledge that Brünnhilde will claim later on. The two may in fact be sharing a moment of syncretic knowledge; if we were to apply a literal temporality to the story's unfolding—as would be appropriate to a police investigation or detective story—we might surmise that Brünnhilde's briefing by the Rhinemaidens would be occurring simultaneously with Siegfried's revelation and death.

Siegfried's recollection of his bond with Brünnhilde, together with his simultaneous realization of his betrayal of her, must, in my own view, be even more catastrophic than his death itself. He is struck by Hagen's spear immediately following this revelation (to him and by him). I suggested to Storey that he might even consider upstaging the event of the fatal stabbing by the experience of knowledge, upstaging the physical trauma by the traumatic revelation. One thing we were all sure of—indeed the topic never came up, so far as I can remember—was that Siegfried would not utter a sound at the moment of the stabbing; he would certainly not scream. The operatic precedent here might be Maria Callas's insistence on the occasion of her studio recording of *Carmen* that she, Callas, would not mark vocally the moment of Carmen's murder—this in disagreement with the producers who held that listeners to the recording, in the absence of visual clues, would require an auditory marking of her stabbing. Similarly, Siegfried's overwhelming revelation must take over his mind and body to the relative devaluation of his own murder. This is part of the shock of the moment, as experienced also by Gunther and the huntsmen. (Storey's success at this moment was confirmed retroactively in later performances. His successor, Andreas Schager, supplied a conventional scream at the moment of the murder—presumably on his own volition and uncorrected by the house directors—and in so doing dissipated a portion of the moment's power and meaning.) The horror of Siegfried's death is that it comes at the very moment when he might have become a hero, a capacity based in his knowledge of the world, himself, and their histories.

Siegfried's death comes, moreover, at the moment of his restored memory. The recollection of his childhood with Mime had never been erased, and its narration comes easily. The return, via a counterpotion again administered by Hagen, of the memory of Brünnhilde is cataclysmic, and must be so to us, the audience, as well. Siegfried's awakening is heralded by the two chords that marked both his awakening of Brünnhilde (in act 3, scene 3 of *Siegfried*) and the opening of *Götterdämmerung* itself. The modulation between them sounds neither a positive signal nor a negative one, but rather a cautionary one that indicates a substantial transformation. Now, for Siegfried, the memory of his awakening of Brünnhilde is simultaneous with the memory and full understanding of his betrayal of her. But there must be more. Siegfried must show us that he knows *everything*—that his never-to-be-realized heroic stature involves the loss of the opportunity to set the world right. Since no performer, and no director, can really hope to impart this kind of tremendous information, the task becomes the function of the orchestral interlude that follows: Siegfried's so-called Funeral March—the dramatic inversion of his first-act Rhine Journey.

The funeral begins necessarily with a procession that removes Siegfried's body from the stage. For its continuation, the video artists Arjen Klerkx and Kurt D'Haeseleer provided projections that proved vague, fleeting, and completely horrifying. Their visual narrative began with a cipher of a lone, slow-moving, oddly distorted, suffering body—almost a cartoon figure but for its gestures of pain and anguish (fig. 4.4). During the Funeral March itself, this image of a suffering body multiplied infinitely, so that the suffering and unjust death of a single figure became the same on an infinite scale: the death of innocence at the scale—cautiously but deliberately invoked—of the Holocaust.

Again and again, in rehearsals and performances in 2013 in both Milan and Berlin, I found myself disturbed, even repulsed, by this odd cartoon image and its uncanny multiplication into figures of mass suffering. It finally struck me as exactly right—this understanding of Siegfried's funeral music as a rage of mourning for a failed dream. This failed dream is the dream of human decency, and therefore the precise opposite of the dream of infinite barbarism that belonged to the Nazis, and according to which they heard and celebrated the same funeral music, including, as is well-known, in a day-long radio loop on the day in April 1945 when Hitler's death had become known. When the Cassiers *Götterdämmerung* was revived in 2016, in Berlin only and presumably for the last time, these images had disappeared.

FIG. 4.4. *Götterdämmerung*, act 3: Siegfried's death. Photo: Koen Broos.

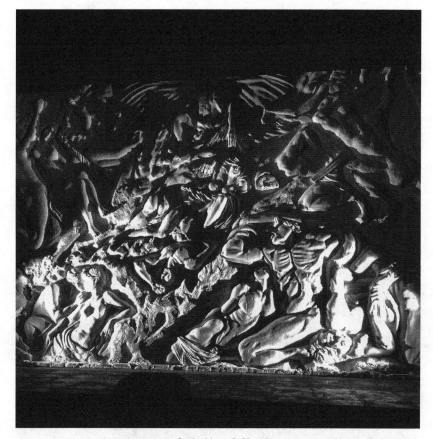

FIG. 4.5. *Götterdämmerung*, final tableau: Jef Lambeaux, *Les passions humaines*. Photo: Michael P. Steinberg.

The mention of Callas returns us briefly to *Norma*. Callas's Norma is consistently cited as the greatest of the age of recorded performance. Her two recordings of the complete opera do justice to the claim on many grounds, from musical accuracy to dramatic intensity to—most difficult to describe—the unique aura she brings to the part. That aura seems always to incorporate silence and mystery, the possibility that beyond all the singing there is, even more significantly, what is not sounded. The Callas aura is about the music, not about the diva. This aura may mark the space of a musical unconscious, and it may indeed accord an unconscious dimension to the character of Norma.

This aura resides beyond the materiality and measurability of the work itself. It respects the "documentary" dimension of the work: the text and the score. It depends on performance but often defies the metrics of performance, forming an additional dimension that the work and its performance together can enable. It emerges unpredictably from fully prepared situations that produce an extra "something," an electricity in which "something happens" which preparation and technique cannot guarantee, an outcome that defies translation into description. Here we arrive back at two moments in this book's introduction. First, the paradoxical identification of *Werktreue*—loyalty to the work—as a kind of impious fidelity: a respect and devotion expressed from within a dynamic of distance, perspective, argument, interpretation. Secondly, the work's capacity for knowledge and self-knowledge—specifically, here, the question as to whether the *Ring* has knowledge of the world as well as of the limitations built into its own magisterial representation of human fallibility. The two issues come together in the generosity of the performative: the capacity of directors, designers, conductors, instrumentalists, and singers to open a space of questioning beyond the work's material content that returns to the work itself the privilege of thinking about itself—to the limit of its own capacity, in other words to the border of its own unconscious (fig. 4.5).

AFTERWORD

On Purity, Danger, and the Postsecular Moment

I

IN A WELL-KNOWN ESSAY OF 1956, JOSEPH KERMAN ARGUED THAT *Tristan und Isolde* should be considered a religious drama, centering on the idea of conversion, rather than a tragedy.[1] Both Tristan and Isolde undergo conversions in the last act, from the cult of love to the cult of death. "Suddenly there is a flood of revelation," Kerman writes, "—that fearful drink: he himself was the one responsible ... and the curse, the purgation, of his own guilt.... Tristan finds in death no longer oblivion, but triumph. ... Isolde's concluding *Liebestod*... achieves the intense, ecstatic concentration on and identification with the ultimate reality of Passion, sharing Tristan's experience from a more inspired standpoint." In citing Kerman, Karol Berger also points out that Michael Tanner and Roger Scruton have made similar arguments.[2] It strikes me that the "religious" is the wrong category here, with its strong implication of the building and the binding of community. The "sacred" (Scruton's correction), with its focus on transcendence, is probably more appropriate to both Tristan's and then Isolde's disavowal of world, day, and society, in favor of eros, night, isolation, and eventually death. The religious, however, is distinctly appropriate to the shape and argument of *Parsifal*, with its explicit portrayal of the community of Monsalvat, at first degraded and finally redeemed. In different ways, *Tristan* and *Parsifal* both point to paths of transcendence of the worldly in ways that the story and music of the *Ring* do not. If the *Ring* is indeed cyclical and not circular, if it does point to some kind of humane future beyond the fall of the gods, it does not define any aspect of that future. In this respect the worldly vision and politics of the *Ring* remain decidedly secular, even materialist, giving substantial authority to Shaw's social reading and its Marxian inspiration.

Tristan—first performed in 1865, prior to the musical composition of act 3 of *Siegfried* and all of *Götterdämmerung*—and *Parsifal*, premiered in Bayreuth in 1882, abjure in their different ways the *Ring*'s worldly focus. For their turns to the sacred, the religious, and the transcendent, these works can be understood not only as examples of what has recently been called the postsecular, but indeed as participants in the invention of the postsecular. Inventing the postsecular, they also reveal the insecurities and dangers of the category itself as a symptom of modern disenchantment.

As a term of advocacy, the "postsecular" has recently come to mark a zone of reappropriation of a religious and communitarian "world we have lost." Its recent literature is both varied and voluminous, ranging from the ever swelling politics of national religious rights, especially in the United States and Europe, to the arguments for pluralistic religious legitimacy. This latter category ranges from a largely majoritarian or Christian perspective (Giorgio Agamben, Slavoj Žižek, Charles Taylor, and Martha Nussbaum, in their significant variety) to a minoritarian and/or Muslim perspective (Talal Asad and Saba Mahmood), to a therapeutic or "psycho-theological" argument (Eric Santner).[3]

Advanced around the turn of the twenty-first century, these varied arguments must perforce take into account the political as well as intellectual upheavals of twentieth-century history. Yet their frames of reference also include, address, and even at times reproduce the nineteenth-century positions that Wagner helped to invent, namely nationalism, mythology, the dialectic of mythology and modernism, and ideologies of blood, including modern racism. Their legacies include capitalism, globalization, late liberalism, cold war, political terrorism, and claims of the end of history. They include also psychoanalysis, existentialism, and postliberal political theory, intellectual categories that invoke the names of Sigmund Freud, Martin Heidegger, and Carl Schmitt. Schmitt's rubric "political theology" is perhaps the most telling intervention for the evolution of the postsecular and its claims. Freud, Heidegger, and Schmitt are all intellectual heirs of Wagner: Freud on the critical/self-critical side; Heidegger and Schmitt on the ideological side. The intellectual history of these legacies would track the afterlife of "Wagner without music"—a topic for another study.

The postsecularities that *Tristan* and *Parsifal* propose differ profoundly. Disavowing the world in favor of a cult of death, *Tristan* follows only its characters into their doomed transcendence. No broader recommendation is suggested. Crucially, for example, King Marke and Brangäne both survive as bystanders, like us, like the anonymous crowd at the end of the *Ring*. As for Tristan himself, there is no better comparison and foil than Siegmund, whose political and generational identity as a child of 1848 is confirmed by a marked secularity. Siegmund's disavowal of Valhalla, his refusal to follow Brünnhilde there, comes from his desire for an earthly life with his partner, Sieglinde. The elements of *Parsifal*'s religious argument are more complex, and indeed more contradictory, involving a radical politics of purification and community. These politics are unavoidably toxic. Yet *Parsifal* too retains a distinct deconstructive element—a voice, literally, of self-critique.

Brünnhilde, as we have seen, disrupts the plot and form of the *Ring* twice. First, she follows Wotan's true will rather than his revised and self-censoring explicit orders. Second, she exposes Siegfried's treachery (alleged or real) while transforming the work in which she appears from music drama to opera—she becomes Norma. Ultimately, however, Wagner, like Wotan, does not cede victory to the transgressive Brünnhilde. Discarding several versions of the text he had written for her, words summarizing her own belated wisdom and the assertion that the world can only be restored through love, he reclaims the hegemonic form of music drama by taking away Brünnhilde's voice and placing his final comment into the merely implicit narrative voice of the orchestra. Six years later he fulfills his own reappropriative campaign with *Parsifal*, the final return of music drama through its own sublimation into the higher sphere of the *Bühnenweihfestspiel* (festival play for the consecration of the stage), a sacred sonic world where no one can have a voice at all, especially the soprano, who loses hers entirely at the end of act 2.[4]

Beyond even the gendering of the voice and the return of sonic authority to the orchestra alone, *Parsifal*'s music is itself constituted as the desire for silence. In musical terms, silence is associated with both completion and death. In plot terms, the desire for death drives two principal protagonists: Amfortas and Kundry, who both live under the curse of unwanted life. Both are guilty of crimes—or rather, sins. Amfortas's sin was the sacrifice of the spiritual in favor of the sensual, the repetition of which Parsifal himself narrowly escapes. Kundry's, more serious and more shocking, was to have witnessed the Crucifixion and laughed. But the desire for silence becomes confused with the violent act of silencing. There is a disingenuousness in this confusion, even a lie. The lie resides in the promise that the world will be reconsecrated, purged of the dissipating demons of modernity. The governing trope of the Holy Grail reinforces the enormousness of the claim: the cup that held the blood of Christ is resanctified along with the world it represents. Christ is himself redeemed, according to the final chorus: "Erlösung dem Erlöser" (Redemption for the Redeemer). The question of what Christ requires redemption from is not answered. The answer may reside in the means of restoration, namely, the cleansing of culture of the element that spilled the blood: the Jews. The Jews, identified literally with bad blood, become the cultural pollutant preventing social reconsecration. *Parsifal*'s claim to restore goodness in fact delivers the world to racism and exclusion. For this reason, contemporary productions have a notoriously difficult time obeying the plot's directives to "allow" both Amfortas and Kundry to die, recipients of the grace of redemption but also the sentence of absolute exclusion from the redeemed community. Wagner's precise stage directions read: "Kundry sinkt, mit dem Blicke zu ihm auf, vor Parsifal entseelt langsam zu Boden" (Kundry sinks, her gaze on Parsifal, soulless to the ground). Wolfgang Wagner in Bayreuth, sensitive perhaps to his grandfather's excesses, had Kundry join the community of the monks. Nikolaus Lehnhoff in Zurich had her accompany all of the monks on a collective march of exile out from Monsalvat.

And yet, ambivalence remains. The leitmotif of the Holy Grail, perhaps the work's most central musical figure, is not original to Wagner but is rather a trope known as the Dresden Amen. Prior to *Parsifal*, it was used as a trope of similar significance in Mendelssohn's *Reformation* Symphony. The upward, longing movement of the phrase can easily be heard as a musical longing for resolution, perhaps specifically the cultural resolution of Jewish assimilation to Christianity. This is presumably how Wagner would have interpreted Mendelssohn's own musically encoded desire. Here as elsewhere, Wagner's conceivable reading would be a mistake, as Mendelssohn's Lutheranism was fully inhabited. For Mendelssohn, the Dresden Amen is a declaration of achieved cultural community. It may retain a motion and emotion of personal desire, but it postdates the achievement of communal integration.

The Dresden Amen appears consistently throughout the course of *Parsifal*, most densely during the act 1 narrative of the faithful monk Gurnemanz as he tells the story of the moral fall of Amfortas at the moment of his seduction by Kundry. But it also appears, ephemerally but to uncanny effect, at a most incongruous moment in act 1, from the mouth of Kundry herself. Moments after her exhausted arrival in the sacred forest and her gift of balsam to the ailing Amfortas, one of Gurnemanz's squires abuses her, asking why she crouches "wie ein wildes Tier" (like a wild animal). Singing the phrase of the Dresden Amen, she replies, with dignity, "Sind die Tiere hier nicht heilig?" (Are the animals not holy here?). The complex utterance indicates her knowledge of Monsalvat, of its codes and rules (setting the stage also for the sacrilegious killing of a swan that will announce Parsifal's arrival). But Wagner here allows Kundry's music to inhabit the musically sacred figure of the Dresden Amen, now associated with the Holy Grail. This may indicate that even she is deserving of redemption, or perhaps, more cynically still, that she knows how to imitate local discourse, the way the most dangerous Jews (according to anti-Semitic claims) are able to pass linguistically as Germans. (This linguistic anxiety is preracist, spurring the racist claim that the body will finally provide the certainty of difference that language was unable to.) But the moment's emotional constitution speaks to a certain sincerity in the work's deployment of the phrase, as if to say, "Listen to this woman!" Wagner does produce Kundry so that he can silence her, but he also wants to listen to her. Here he himself resembles the Wanderer (Wotan) in act 3 of *Siegfried*, awakening his consort Erda so that he can order her to go back to sleep. Erda and Kundry share a kind of forbidden wisdom, and the Wanderer and Wagner alike betray their own desire to proceed—in the words of the Norns—"hinab ... zur Mutter" (down ... to the mother). Kundry is both fallen woman and wandering Jew. By allowing her—however momentarily—to speak, and to speak truth, Wagner enters the aporia in his own ideological apparatus. In a flash of uncanny self-disclosure, he becomes the wandering Jew Mendelssohn (as he described him in *Judaism in Music*) so that he might listen to the wandering Jewess Kundry.

Amfortas's wound is the condition of modernity. The closing of the wound—the promise of *Parsifal* and Parsifal—amounts to the end of pain and the end of history, and also to the end of music and the end of listening. Amfortas's wound is of the body and body politic in the same way that the voice is of the body. The curse and promise of modernity, however, is the need for subjectivity to reconstitute itself continuously. In this respect, the bureaucratic mentality is the enemy of a mobile, imaginative subjectivity. The modern ego both seeks recognition in a sense of belonging and at the same time rebels against the kinds of belonging that absorb too much of the ego and its fragile potential of autonomy. Secular autonomy wants freedom on earth, as Siegmund instructs Brünnhilde. In a bureaucratic context, the modern ego may feel recognized by placement in a formal, professional, or indeed ritual position. The basic German word for "profession" is *Beruf*, which preserves etymologically the sacred idea of the calling, as Max Weber affirmed. But the modern ego also rebels against the command to be *am Amt* (at one's post, on the job). When being *am Amt* is confused with a surfeit of solidarity (in Émile Durkheim's sense of the integration of the self with the community), with an evacuation of the ego, then the inability to be *am Amt* is the anomic wound of the pariah. To be *am Amt* means to be a *Beamter*, a functionary, to participate in the self-sacrifice of subjectivity. The collective anomie of modernity is the wound that anti-Semitism blames on the Jews. Amfortas's inability to perform his duty is the refusal to be *am Amt*, the refusal he expresses to his father, Titurel. Titurel, in turn, has no patience with his son's personal crisis, or with his symptomatizing of a modern crisis, for that matter. Amfortas exemplifies the Wilhelmine son: the incapacitated, oversensitive heir to a *grossbürgerlich* father, titan, regent: Max Weber, Daniel Paul Schreber, Aby Warburg, Frederick III of Prussia, Crown Prince Rudolf of Austria. This generation suffers from a burden that their fathers didn't have: the command to choose an identity and a way of living correlative to and compatible with the official culture of the German Empire. Masculinity and respectability are now no longer civic virtues but imperial ones.

Amfortas's alienation, however, is not only generational. It is also cultural. Like Wagner himself, Amfortas is out of place as a Saxon Protestant trapped in a Catholic baroque play. His refusal to perform the ritual of the Grail must be taken seriously not merely as a sign of incompetence but as the very refusal of theatricality. In this *Bühnenweihfestspiel*, it is the stage, the *Bühne*, to which he objects most. Living with the wound as an aspect of sensation and interiority, he refuses to honor its visual correlative in the (bleeding) vessel, the Grail itself. (Wagner followed the false etymology of the word "grail" as a conflation of *sang réal* [royal blood].) The evolution of German Protestantism, as Heinz-Dieter Kittsteiner and others have argued, corresponds to the internalization of conscience and the increasing suspicion of representation.[5] For Mary Douglas, the Protestant rejection of magic as a kind of repetition of the ancient Hebrew rejection of paganism included also the English and Scots: "In a sense magic was to the Hebrews what Catholicism was to the Protestants, mumbo-jumbo, meaningless ritual, irrationally held to be sufficient in itself to produce results without an inner experience of God."[6] Interiority resists mimetic display; the wound cannot be represented. Titurel wants to *see* the Grail. In his father's house, Amfortas's duty to care for the Grail, which he wants to disavow, is identical to its visualization, to its revelation ("Enthülle den Grail!" [Reveal the Grail!]). At the Berlin State Opera (2016), Dmitri Tcherniakov had the monks become abusive to Amfortas, unwrapping his bandages in the demand to see the wound, as if to confuse it with the Grail itself as a carrier of holy blood. Here and generally, the suffering Amfortas recoils from the demands of the theater, from the spotlight—*Lichtstrahl*—that descends onto the ritual object. Thus the passage from father Titurel to son Amfortas embodies the passage from mid-century grand bourgeois to fin-de-siècle decadent, but it reinscribes as well the early history of modernity, which German historiography consistently places in the passage from Catholicism to Protestantism, from ritual magic to human isolation from the divine, from ideologies of seeing to subversive, invisible interiorities: regimes of the ear and the wound.

The early Protestants' assertion of human isolation from the divine enabled, unintentionally, the take-off of the secular. Such is the argument of Max Weber's aporetic masterpiece *The Protestant Ethic and the Spirit of Capitalism*, with its definition of modernity, taken ultimately from Friedrich Schiller, as the disenchantment of the world. Weber began work on this project upon his emergence from the years of psychic dysfunction that followed the death of his father. He thus lived the modern disenchantment through which the fin-de-siècle generation recapitulated the general history of modernity. The tragic irony of the modern—the iron cage, in Weber's formulation—is disenchantment's simultaneous restoration of interiority and its second loss through rationalization and bureaucracy.

As in the case of the repeated subjection of Brünnhilde—by Wotan, by Siegfried, by Wagner—music drama ends up a symptom of the bureaucratic side of modernity. Music drama rationalizes and systematizes the transgressive energy of opera and the voice. Leitmotivic writing becomes— or, rather, can become—composition by administration, especially in the scholarship that takes von Wolzogen's catalog of leitmotifs as a guide to music and music drama. Against this pressure, the voice remains the instrument of the siren and the prophet, of both truth and hallucination. It is also the voice of the citizen, the voice of the individual's disclosure to the polis, in Hannah Arendt's formulation. Max Weber's reclassification of the prerationalized and the rationalized modes of political power into the charismatic and the bureaucratic carries as well his own political and theoretical refusal to choose between charisma and bureaucracy as the bearers of political legitimacy. As he decries the iron cage of law and bureaucracy, he prepares himself to reenter the public sphere as a framer of the Weimar constitution. At the traumatic moment of transition from empire to republic, Weber is again *am Amt*. The refusal to choose between charisma and bureaucracy includes the refusal to produce their synthesis, their resolution, their transcendence. Weber died suddenly in 1920. It would be useful to rehistoricize the long Weimar decade of 1920 to 1933 as the struggle between Weberian principles and Wagnerism.

Parsifal's is a politics of purity and purification, amounting more or less to our contemporary category of ethnic cleansing. The argument is unavoidably internal to the work. Here the work's unique performance history comes into play as well. To underscore the sanctity of *Parsifal* as a *Bühnenweihfestspiel*, Wagner instructed in his will that it be performed — or rather, celebrated — only in Bayreuth. This triple consecration — of the work itself, of the house of Bayreuth, and of the German nation, now an empire — statutorily combined ethnic cleansing with nationalism and imperialism. Following his death in 1883, six months after the premiere of *Parsifal*, Cosima Wagner enforced her husband's wish with ferocity until the Metropolitan Opera challenged her in 1903 (citing the United States twenty-year statute of limitations from the date of Wagner's death) in an assault on the Grail that Cosima attributed to the Jewish origin of its general manager, Heinrich Conreid, né Cohn.[7]

"Danger," Mary Douglas writes in her classic study *Purity and Danger*, "lies in marginal states." Douglas cites Arnold van Gennep for the "sociological insight" that understood society itself "as a house with rooms and corridors in which passage from one to another is dangerous. Danger lies in transitional states, simply because transition is neither one state nor the next, it is undefinable. The person who must pass from one to another is himself in danger and emanates danger to others. The danger is controlled by ritual which precisely separates him from his old status, segregates him for a time and then publicly declares his entry to his new status."[8] This is the kind of portentous transition that Gurnemanz has in mind when he decides to guide the *enfant sauvage* Parsifal to Monsalvat with the words "Du siehst mein Sohn: zum Raum wird hier die Zeit" (You see, my son, here time becomes space). Claude Lévi-Strauss characterized this moment as "probably the most profound definition that anyone has ever offered for myth."[9] For Douglas, presumably, the achievement of myth would be the goal or wish of the transitional state: the achievement of space and stability as the resolution of time and flux. In musical terms, again, this is the "achievement" of silence as the mark of resolution. The pulse of history, however, is marked by the continuity of transitional states, thus the etymology of the word "secular": ordinary, earthly time. The "end of history" is itself a myth of resacralization, on the way to which the "postsecular" is presumably the final stage of transition. At the same time, we can define the postsecular as the disenchantment with disenchantment, in other words as a fundamentally secular phenomenon itself.

With *Parsifal*, Wagner stands as a prime inventor of the postsecular.

Tristan's hint in that direction, if we follow Kerman, remains palpable but nonviable, as it ends only in personal death. The *Ring*, in its inscription of history as cyclical or circular, defies such sacralization or resacralization. Siegmund's crime—and the motivator of the punishment that cannot be countermanded for fear of social collapse—involves the multiple taboos of social marginality and instability: adultery, incest, and perhaps Jewishness, as we saw in chapter 2.

2

When Bronislav Huberman, the founder of the Palestine Symphony, persuaded Arturo Toscanini to conduct its inaugural concerts in Tel Aviv in December 1936, they placed the prelude to Wagner's *Die Meistersinger von Nürnberg* on the program. Some three thousand people attended, including the British High Commissioner, Arthur Wauchope; Chaim Weizmann; David Ben-Gurion; Golda Meir; and Tel Aviv's first mayor, Meir Dizengoff. In December 1938 the orchestra removed the same piece from a concert program in the aftermath of the *Kristallnacht* terror of November 9. That gesture held. In the period following the Holocaust, the declaration of the state of Israel in 1948, and the transition of the Palestine Symphony into the Israel Philharmonic, the public performance of Wagner in Israel solidified as a cultural taboo that has only intensified over time, extending to several failed proposals to the Knesset to elevate the ban into national law.[10] Carefully calibrated attempts by Daniel Barenboim, Zubin Mehta, and the Israel Philharmonic to introduce Wagner to local audiences in small and nonpolitical doses (with music from *Tristan und Isolde* offered as optional encores to nonsubscription concerts) have failed to gain traction owing to extensive post facto publicity and opposition. The taboo is kept alive by several factors: by the correct identification of Wagner with the onset of racialized anti-Semitism; by the dubious association of Wagner with the Third Reich (often grounded in the false assertion of their simultaneity); and by the citation of and respect for traumatic repetition on the part of survivors who, correctly or not, associate Wagner with the Holocaust. The extreme (and largely authoritative) imposition of the taboo demands that this music not be played in any form, live or recorded, anywhere in the country. This position abandons cultural negotiation in favor of a ban on desecration or pollution of a sacred space.

More generally, however, the anxiety over race and racial thinking in Wagner and beyond amounts to an anxiety about the sources and boundaries of identity and selfhood—the individual self and also the collective or indeed national self. Wagner's musical-dramatic world, replete though it may be with racist thinking and even stereotyping, contains an equally powerful deconstructive element that displaces such ideology with a convincing foray into critical and self-critical depths. (The self-criticism I refer to here emerges at the level of the work, not the man—and in the music dramas, not the essays.) That duality has been this book's principal argument. Wagner's musical, dramatic, and critical depths are both experiential and analytical. If Beethoven freed music, Wagner took music into the depths of the unconscious, the forbidden dimension of the human psyche that artists recognized, as Freud said, before he mapped it scientifically. Because it is a driver of both knowledge and violence, the unconscious is dangerous. Wagner's music is thus equally dangerous for what it finds there, what it duplicates, and what it handles critically. Wagner occupies both sides of modernism: the absolutist side, which in his case begins with the "absolute music" (a term, again, that he coined) of Beethoven and metastasizes into fantasies of absolute myth and absolute culture; and the critical, deconstructive side, which drives meaning and knowledge according to expectations of multiplicity and infinite variation. If music drama shows the capacity to engage the unconscious, as I argued in chapter 3, it also *has* an unconscious. Music drama's unconscious is, to be totally short, opera—the place and forms in which its own deconstructive capacities take flight.

Does the Israeli taboo have an unconscious? The taboo can be understood in understood in two dimensions, reacting to the two dimensions of Wagner. First and openly, the taboo universalizes and rejects Wagner's anti-Semitism, painting it with too broad and monotonic a brush. But, second, the taboo results, I would argue, from an inadequate and anxious response to the challenge that Wagner's self-critical, deconstructive energy poses to the very arguments of sacralization, and specifically to the resacralization of modernity and modern societies. In this sense, the taboo's unconscious involves an anxiety about the nonviability of the sacred community in which the very idea of the state of Israel is grounded. To be sure, the taboo is neither generated nor safeguarded by Israeli listeners with a deep or sustained engagement with Wagner and his intricacies. But even the simplest avoidance of the music hears in it a disruptive capacity, and the question follows quickly as to what is being disrupted.

Just as much as Wagner's construction of the postsecular, it is his critique which proves a threat to mainstream Israeli discourse, its guardianship of the Wagner taboo, and its insistence on a social foundation of religious exclusivity. Wagner the outsider, not the insider, proves dangerous here: Siegmund, not Parsifal. The Wagner taboo emerges as a symptom of anxiety about the nation itself: in this case, the national self that wishes to equate the Israeli with the Jewish as authentic and equal marks of citizenship, despite the multiple historical and legal impediments to that desire, including the legal citizenship of the Palestinian citizens of Israel who make up 20 percent of the population. This imagined community would wish to transcend the political, itself understood as the continuous negotiation of instabilities, margins, and transitions. Here as elsewhere, the instability in Wagner threatens more than the ideology. And specifically, the inner tensions and contradictions, the recognitions of reality, ambiguity, and danger, emerge more sharply than the claim of cultural purity, which remains the gravest political danger of all.

3

The antidote to that claim and its dangers, weakening transatlantically and indeed globally as I write these last lines in late 2017, is the secular social contract, based in plurality and reciprocation. In a transitional and fleeting scene in act 1 of *Die Meistersinger*, Wagner lets us into a quotidian articulation of such a contract, short-lived as its mood may prove prior to its displacement by the oceanic powers (*Wahn*) of both art and violence.

The mastersingers assemble for their weekly meeting and announce their presence to their secretary, the baker Fritz Kothner, to a stepwise progression of the motif associated with the mastersingers in their daily *non*musical professions. It accompanies in particular Veit Pogner, goldsmith and father of the heroine-to-be, Eva. The sequence resounds with a sense of collective presence whose appeal to me has always surprised me. I have always heard it as a healthy display of dignity and self-awareness, distinctly short of pomp and self-importance. The sequence sounds to me like the acknowledgment and even the enactment of citizenship, the performance of *Bürgerlichkeit*. Its music makes me feel the meaning of the gestures I want to see onstage: the pleasure of association and reunion, of leaning forward in greeting, of the shaking or double-clasping of hands and nodding of heads. These are the gestures, the body language, the *Bürgerlichkeit*, the solid citizenship I recall from my childhood observations of my grandparents' generation, reduced by age and émigré status but nevertheless both dignified and affirmed by their sociability. Here the names Konrad Nachtigall, Ulrich Esslinger, Hermann Ortel, and Augustin Moser are replaced (it's a pleasure to recall and inscribe these names) by Max Steinberg, Max Hoffman, Fritz (Siegfried) Oppenheimer, Ernst Levisohn, Sigmar Günzburger, Isidore Guggenheim, and Sigl (Siegfried) Weil. Refugees and elderly men when I knew them, they assembled in Fort Tryon Park in upper Manhattan with the same body language, the same performance of dignity and association, that Wagner recognized in the burghers of the 1860s and projected back onto his early sixteenth-century characters.

But if affectionate sociability defines one side of German *Bürgerlichkeit*, the upholding of convention often defines the other. Social insecurity easily encourages this other side, including or even especially in the context of German Jewish history. The elderly refugees of my grandparents' generation whom I remember from my childhood were thrust out of their conventions and forced to reinvent their lives. Such is an education in both courage and imagination. The mastersingers of Wagner's act 1, capacious as they seem in the forming of bonds across boundaries of profession and conceivably, confession, conclude their session by brutalizing the experimental artist, Walther von Stolzing, in the name of cultural solidarity, tradition, and the rules of their game. The negotiation of tradition and innovation thus becomes a principal thematic thread of the opera. Von Stolzing's aesthetic education, under the tutelage of Hans Sachs, masters the dialectic and finally wins over the skeptical mastersingers. At the conclusion of act 3, the stage directions are explicit: the mastersingers have been handed the text of Walther's prize song (let's leave aside the problem of when it might have been copied!), and, in their rapture, release the paper into the wind at the moment Walther begins to improvise on the song that we, the audience, have now heard twice through. As a whole and by its end, act 3 of *Die Meistersinger* produces and performs movingly the redemption of the aesthetic and erotic imagination, while foreclosing entirely on its own claim of integrating eros and improvisation into its newly imagined national community. The conclusion is terrifying.

ACKNOWLEDGMENTS

Without any doubt this book traces its start to a Monday in early August, 1976, when two of us student travelers gained unexpected access to the second performance of Patrice Chéreau's Bayreuth *Götterdämmerung*. Pierre Boulez was in the pit, Roberta Knie sang Brünnhilde, the audience was in high agitation, and after the long first act we ran to each other from our separate seats knowing that this event would prove life-changing, maybe for Wagner, certainly for us. Before that, however, there was the Metropolitan Opera's neo-Wieland Wagner *Tristan* in November 1971 (August Everding and Günter Schneider-Siemssen; Erich Leinsdorf; Birgit Nilsson and Jess Thomas): a modernist icon of a production that holds up uncannily in my memories of high-school-days opera discovery in New York. That discovery was enabled by the Birch Wathen School and an underused educational subscription to the Metropolitan Opera Guild. Our redoubtable school secretary Miss McDow, a native Oklahoman of infinite operatic refinement, would request and didactically dispense fifth-balcony side seats (at $2.85) and score desks without visibility (at $1.50) to two interested students and a slightly larger cohort of teachers. Miss McDow knew how much we appreciated her.

The book itself and its double genealogy owe much to key interlocutors. Daniel Herwitz continues to be my thinking alter ego after close to four decades. Wendy Doniger, with whom I taught a class titled "Opera, Myth, History" at the University of Chicago in 1995, continues to spar with me about the boundaries between myth and history. My circle of Wagnerians *malgré nous-mêmes* begins with David Levin, whose unique alchemy of insight and indignation, together with the key conference he ran at Columbia University in November 1995, continues to set the tone. To David I owe my friendship with Pamela Rosenberg, former Intendant of the Frankfurt, Stuttgart, and San Francisco Operas and the Berlin Philharmonic, and later dean of Fellows at the American Academy in Berlin. Co-teaching one of my Brown University Wagner seminars for a month in 2006, Pamela once advised a student with a detailed question about Wotan's kiss to Brünnhilde in the Stuttgart *Walküre* simply to write to the director and ask him about it.

I first met Daniel Barenboim through the generosity of my local mentor, Michael Blumenthal, during my 2003 fellowship period at the American Academy in Berlin; my working relationship with him I owe to Pamela. It has three parts. Wagner—and this book—trace the first dimension. It was sparked by a conversation in late 2008, when he told me that La Scala had engaged Guy Cassiers to direct the new *Ring*, and that the team would welcome some input about the nineteenth century generally and about the *Ring*'s production history more specifically. We all first met together in February 2009, fifteen months before the scheduled premiere of *Das Rheingold*. The second dimension involves the West-Eastern Divan Orchestra, which Barenboim founded with Edward Said in 1999. In 2006 and again in 2013 I was able to bring the full orchestra to Brown for residencies that included concerts and discussions of political and cultural encounters across difficult lines of communication. My summers from 2008 through 2011 involved several periods with the orchestra during their rehearsal and discussion residencies in Andalusia, accompanied by some of my own students. In 2008 Barenboim's challenge to the young Jews and Arabs of the Divan was to have them play Wagner together: the complete first act of *Die Walküre*. Multiple boundaries were crossed: the Israelis played Wagner; the Jews and Arabs played Wagner together; and the orchestra took on a complete operatic act for the first time. Patrice Chéreau was nearby, and the three of us convened a panel about his now legendary 1976 production. An assistant conductor asked us, guilelessly, "What does the *Ring* have to do with the nineteenth century?" During these summers as well, Barenboim, Pamela, Carsten Siebert, and I sat together—occasionally alongside such key musician-mentors as the Berliner Staatskapelle concertmaster, Axel Wilczok, and the principal clarinetist, Mathias Glander—to begin to draft a humanities curriculum for the projected Barenboim-Said Akademie in Berlin. This institution is now newly inaugurated, its evolving music and humanities curriculum in the hands of able, creative leadership. Said's germinal notion of "music education" becoming "education through music" lives, at a key moment in time and in the best place and space for it in the world.

The book's completion carries happy debts to the Humanities Research Centre at the Australian National University and to the Wissenschaftskolleg zu Berlin, where a fellowship enabled me to work for three months during a period that overlapped with rehearsals for the June 2016 Berlin revival of the Barenboim-Cassiers *Ring*. At the Berlin State Opera I am deeply grateful to Daniel Barenboim and also to Jürgen Flimm, Detlev Giese, Derek Gimpel, and Antje Werkmeister. And at La Scala, to Stéphane Lissner, Franco Pulcini, and, most especially, Gaston Fournier-Facio, whose hospitality extended to a group of ten Brown University students during a course-related trip to Milan and stage rehearsals for *Das Rheingold* in May 2010. In Milan and Berlin, and always first through multiple meetings in their home city of Antwerp, Guy Cassiers and Adrienne Altenhaus, the designer Enrico Bagnoli, the video artists Arjen Klerkx and Kurt D'Haeseleer, the costume designer Tim van Steenbergen, and the entire Toneelhuis team brought me into a conversation at once intellectually familiar and contextually completely new. The Toneelhuis's practice of adapting canonic works from Proust to Musil to Lowry into lean, kinetic stage productions exemplifies the kind of interventionary curation that grounds not only the vision of Wagner's *Ring* in play here, but also my own arguments about Wagner and the interfaces between past and present, form and history.

The 2010 student trip to Milan was followed by similar programs in Berlin between 2011 and 2014, guided by Adam J. Sacks and later by Leslie Uhnak, the magical and deeply missed academic coordinator of Brown's Cogut Center for the Humanities. A truly generous spirit, Leslie opened this operatic world for the students as she discovered it herself. The Cogut Center's Kit Salisbury, Traude Kastner, and, earlier, Keith Brown were equally fundamental to these initiatives, as they had been in convening the two conferences "Unsettling Opera" (February 2006) and "Wagner and Scandal" (March 2008) alongside scholars and practitioners including David Levin and Pamela Rosenberg as well as Lydia Goehr, John Rockwell, Peter Sellars, Emanuele Senici, Robert Sollich, and many others. As my intellectual home for a decade, the Cogut Center enabled the kind of rigorous, worldly mix of curation and innovation that the book depends on. On U.S. university campuses, humanities centers and institutes alone play this role. A semester's leave from Brown in 2013 allowed me to participate in sustained rehearsals of *Götterdämmerung* in Berlin far more fully than I had been able to over the course of the three previous works' rehearsal periods, an advantage that inflects the discussion in chapter 6.

At the University of Chicago Press, Marta Tonegutti and two superbly selected referees guided the manuscript with insight into Wagner, Wagner studies, as well as the general claims and practices of the cultural history and analysis of music.

I dedicate the book to my family. Though the musical tastes of my children, Daniel and daughter-in-law Mary, Andrew, Jamie, and Anna, largely bypass my own, their affective and political convictions—as well as the links between these and music itself—do not. My family has sustained me always, and most fundamentally during the period of illness that coincided with the preparation of this book. From this unexpected and life-changing context specifically, I offer tribute to my mother, Suzanne Steinberg, whose voice and counsel remain as indispensable to me as ever; to my sister, Vivian Cohn, whose presence and steadfastness are absolute; and overwhelmingly to my wife Katy, who has turned daily life—most especially but not only during a period of severe restrictions—into the everyday sublime.

NOTES

INTRODUCTION

1. See Daniel Barenboim, "Wagner, Israel, and the Palestinians," www.danielbarenboim.com.
2. Philip Kitcher and Richard Schacht, *Finding an Ending: Reflections on Wagner's "Ring"* (Oxford: Oxford University Press, 2004), 4.
3. Shulamit Volkov, *Antisemitismus als kultureller Code* (Munich: C. H. Beck Verlag, 2000).
4. D. W. Winnicott, *Playing and Reality* (London: Routledge, 1982).
5. Friedrich Nietzsche, *The Case of Wagner*, trans. W. Kaufmann (New York: Vintage, 1967), 161.
6. The Prussian legal code (Allgemeine Landrecht für die preussischen Staaten) of 1794 identified the status of intersexed persons in the section that became known as the *Zwitterparagraph*. It recommended that parents decide on gender identity. The paragraph was revoked in 1875. In late 2017 the German Federal Constitutional Court ruled for the legal recognition of a third gender/sex category marked as either "inter" or "diverse."
7. Carl Dahlhaus, *Richard Wagner's Music Dramas*, trans. Mary Whittall (Cambridge: Cambridge University Press, 1979), 4–6.
8. See David Trippett, *Wagner's Melodies: Aesthetics and Materialism in German Musical Identity* (Cambridge: Cambridge University Press, 2013).
9. This was the topic and argument of my earlier book *Listening to Reason: Culture, Subjectivity, and Nineteenth-Century Music* (Princeton, NJ: Princeton University Press, 2004).
10. The symbol of the swan for Luther likely originates in a story about Jan Hus, the Czech reformer burned at the stake for heresy in 1415. At his execution he is reported to have exclaimed, "You are now going to burn a goose, but in a century you will have a swan which you can neither roast nor boil." And on the night prior to October 31, 1517, Elector Frederick of Saxony is said to have reported a dream of a priest who wrote on the doors of the Wittenberg Cathedral with a large pen that had belonged to a goose of Bohemia. That day, Luther posted there his *Ninety-five Theses*. (See these stories at lutheranpress.com.) Finally, the fall 2017 exhibition "The Luther Effect: Protestantism—500 Years in the World," curated by the Deutsches Historisches Museum at the Martin-Gropius-Bau, Berlin, displayed a weathervane from the Evangelical Reformed

Church in Groothusen on the North Sea coast, dated 1597, in the form of a golden (copper-gilded) "Luther Swan."

11. Lucien Febvre, *The Problem of Unbelief in the Sixteenth Century: The Religion of Rabelais* (Cambridge, MA: Harvard University Press, 1985).

12. Svetlana Boym, *The Future of Nostalgia* (New York: Basic Books, 2002).

13. See Claude Lévi-Strauss, *Myth and Meaning: Cracking the Code of Culture* (New York: Schocken Books, 1995), 12.

14. Ruth Berghaus, interview of December 5, 1985, included in the exhibition of Wagner's scenic designs, *Wagner 2013: Künstler, Positionen*, curated by Nele Hertling, Reinhild Hoffmann, Thomas Langhoff, Sven Neumann, Akademie der Künste Berlin, December 2012–February 2013.

15. Adam Phillips, *Missing Out: In Praise of the Unlived Life* (New York: Farrar, Straus & Giroux, 2013), 54.

16. Ibid., 74.

17. Adam Phillips, "Winnicott's Hamlet," in *Promises, Promises* (New York: Basic Books, 2009).

18. Carolyn Abbate, *Unsung Voices: Opera and Musical Narrative in the Nineteenth Century* (Princeton, NJ: Princeton University Press, 1991), 161. See also David J. Levin, *Richard Wagner, Fritz Lang, and the Nibelungen* (Princeton, NJ: Princeton University Press, 1998), especially chap. 2, "Where Narration Was, There *Darstellung* Shall Be: Wagner and the Scene of Narration," 30–95.

19. Hermann Broch, *Hugo von Hofmannsthal and His Time* (Chicago: University of Chicago Press, 1984), chap. 1, esp. 49.

20. Bruce Chatwin, *The Songlines* (New York: Penguin Books, 1987), 56–57. Ten pages further on in his idiosyncratic account of aboriginal cosmology, Chatwin discusses briefly the work of T. G. H. (Ted) Strehlow, including *Aranda Traditions* (1947), a study of "primitive" intellect that, according to Chatwin, Claude Lévi-Strauss incorporated into the argument of *The Savage Mind*, and especially *Songs of Central Australia* (1971). Strehlow's father, Karl, Chatwin recounts, "had been pastor in charge of the Lutheran Mission at Hermannsburg.... one of a handful of 'good Germans' who, by providing a secure land-base, did more than anyone to save the Central Australian Aboriginals from extinction by people of British stock. This did not make him popular. During the First World War, a press campaign broke out against the 'Teuton spies' nest' and the 'evil effects of Germanising the natives.'" Conceivably—though this is not Chatwin's implication—Ted Strehlow's ethnography and ethnomusicology might also prove vulnerable to the accusation of Germanising native forms and practices. Strehlow, reports Chatwin, "once compared the study of Aboriginal myths to entering a 'labyrinth of countless corridors and passages.'" The apt question, then, might be whether his engagement is more Wagnerian or Wolzogenesque; Chatwin, *Songlines*, 68, 69, 70. More recent scholarship on Australian aboriginal culture has argued for the syncretism of cosmology, visuality, song, and dance combining to form songlines as both markers and actual creations or recreations of ancestrally marked landscapes. See Diana James, *Painting the Song: Kaltjiti Artists of the Sand Dune Country* (Fitzroy, Victoria: McCulloch & McCulloch Australian Art Books, 2009); Howard Morphy, *Aboriginal Art* (London:

Phaidon Press, 1998); Gordon Kalton Williams, "Meetings Centrestage," in *Spirit of the Land* 3:1999 (Byron Bay, NSW: Spirit of the Land Foundation) for an account of a cooperative venture between the Adelaide Symphony Orchestra and Aboriginal music makers called "Orchestra Dreaming."

21. See Lévi-Strauss, *Myth and Meaning*, 40.

CHAPTER 1

1. Karl Marx, *The German Ideology* (1844).
2. Francesco Galeazzi, *Elementi teorico-practici di musica* (1796), as translated into English in Rita Steblin, *A History of Key Characteristics in the Eighteenth and Early Nineteenth Centuries* (Rochester, NY: University of Rochester Press, 1996), 111. Thanks to Karol Berger for this reference.
3. Theodor Adorno, *In Search of Wagner* (London: Verso Books, 2005), 72.
4. Ibid., 66–67, 68.
5. Lévi-Strauss, *Myth and Meaning*, 8.
6. Robert Donington, *Wagner's "Ring" and Its Symbols: The Music and the Myth* (New York: St. Martin's Press, 1974).
7. George Bernard Shaw, *The Perfect Wagnerite: A Commentary on the Niblung's Ring*. Online access via Project Gutenberg, www.gutenberg.org.
8. The Leipzig *Ring* was highlighted in the bicentennial exhibition *Wagner: Künstlerpositionen*, Akademie der Künste, Berlin, December 2012–February 2013.
9. G. E. Lessing, *Laocoön: An Essay on the Limits of Painting and Poetry*, trans. E. A. McCormick (Baltimore, MD: Johns Hopkins University Press, 1984).
10. Hannah Arendt, *The Origins of Totalitarianism* (New York: Harvest Books, 1968), 188–89.
11. Adam Hochschild, *King Leopold's Ghost: A Story of Greed, Terror, and Heroism in Colonial Africa* (New York: Mariner Books, 1998).
12. Debora L. Silverman, "*Modernité sans frontières*: Culture, Politics, and the Boundaries of the Avant-Garde in King Leopold's Belgium, 1885–1910," *American Imago* 68, no. 4 (2012): 738.
13. Debora L. Silverman, "Art Nouveau, Art of Darkness: African Lineages of Belgian Modernism, Part III," *West 86th* 20, no. 1 (2013): 26.
14. Silverman, "*Modernité sans frontières*," 778.
15. Silverman, "Art Nouveau," 45.
16. Slavoj Žižek, "Why Is Wagner Worth Saving?," foreword to Theodor Adorno, *In Search of Wagner* (London: Verso Books, 2009), xviii.
17. I owe this insight into the second meaning of *gleich* to one of the anonymous referees of the manuscript.

CHAPTER 2

1. David Warren Sabean, "Fanny and Felix Mendelssohn-Bartholdy and the Question of Incest," *Musical Quarterly* 77, no. 4 (Winter 1993): 712.
2. Thomas Mann, "The Blood of the Walsungs," in *Death in Venice and Seven Other Stories*, trans. H. T. Lowe-Porter (New York: Vintage Books, 1954), 309.

3. The remark is also cited by Patrice Chéreau in his memoir of his production of the *Ring* for the Bayreuth Festival. See Chéreau, *Lorsque cinq ans seront passés* (Toulouse: Éditions Ombres, 1994), 17.

4. Sigmund Freud, "The Case of the Wolf-Man," in *The Wolf Man*: The Double Story of Freud's Most Famous Case (New York: Basic Books, 1971).

5. Karol Berger, *Beyond Reason: Wagner contra Nietzsche* (Berkeley and Los Angeles: University of California Press, 2017), 54.

6. See Peter Conrad, *Richard Wagner: Romantic Opera and Literary Form* (Berkeley and Los Angeles: University of California Press, 1977).

CHAPTER 3

1. Jürgen Habermas, *Structural Transformation of the Public Sphere* (Cambridge, MA: MIT Press, 1962).

2. Bruce Chatwin, *The Songlines* (New York: Penguin Books, 1987), 219.

3. Sigmund Freud, *Neue Folge der Vorlesungen zur Einführung in die Psychoanalyse* (1933); translated into English as *New Introductory Lectures on Psycho-Analysis* (New York: Norton, 1990).

4. For an exhaustive and hospitable catalogue of leitmotifs, including short mp3 audio files, go to www.pjb.com.au and open "The Leitmotifs of Wagner's *Ring*." Click on d8 for the Ring motif and on d57 for the Dragon motif.

5. Wendy Doniger, *The Ring of Truth: And Other Myths of Sex and Jewelry* (Oxford and New York: Oxford University Press, 2017), chap. 5, "Siegfried's Ring and Wagner's Ring."

6. Friedrich Nietzsche, *Beyond Good and Evil: Prelude to a Philosophy of the Future*, trans. Walter Kaufmann (New York: Vintage, 1966), aphorism 254, p. 195.

7. Shaw, *The Perfect Wagnerite*.

CHAPTER 4

1. See John Louis DeGaetani, *Richard Wagner and the Modern British Novel* (London: Associated University Presses, 1978), 25–26.

2. Isabel V. Hull, *Absolute Destruction: Military Culture and the Practices of War in Imperial Germany* (Ithaca, NY: Cornell University Press, 2005), 1 and *passim*.

3. Hochschild, *King Leopold's Ghost*, 1 and passim.

4. Nietzsche, *Beyond Good and Evil*.

AFTERWORD

1. Joseph Kerman, "*Tristan und Isolde*: The Prelude and the Play," in *Write All These Down: Essays on Music* (Berkeley and Los Angeles: University of California Press, 1994), 335–49. See also Berger, *Beyond Reason*, 234.

2. Michael Tanner, "The Passion of Passion," in *Wagner* (Princeton, NJ: Princeton University Press, 1996), 140–55; Roger Scruton, *Death-Devoted Heart: Sex and the Sacred in Wagner's "Tristan and Isolde"* (New York: Oxford University Press, 2004).

3. For a critique of the political slippage among advocates of postsecular argument,

see Stathis Gourgouris, *Lessons in Secular Criticism* (New York: Columbia University Press, 2014).

4. See Suzanne R. Stewart, *Sublime Surrender: Male Masochism at the Fin-de-Siècle* (Ithaca, NY: Cornell University Press, 1998), chap. 3, "The Theft of the Operatic Voice: Masochistic Seduction in Wagner's *Parsifal*," 89–115.

5. Heinz-Dieter Kittsteiner, *Die Entstehung des modernen Gewissens* (Frankfurt am Main: Insel Verlag, 1991).

6. Mary Douglas, *Purity and Danger: An Analysis of Concepts of Pollution and Taboo* (London: Routledge & Kegan Paul, 1966), 18.

7. See Robert Gutman, *Richard Wagner: The Man, His Mind, and His Music* (New York: Harvest, 1966), 409. There were several isolated European performances outside of Bayreuth prior to 1903. See Barry Millington, "Parsifal," in *The New Grove Dictionary of Opera*, 3rd ed. (London: Macmillan, 1992), 891.

8. Douglas, *Purity and Danger*, 97.

9. Claude Lévi-Strauss, "From Chrétien de Troyes to Richard Wagner," in *The View from Afar* (New York: Basic Books, 1985), 219.

10. The taboo is well chronicled in Na'ama Sheffi, *The Ring of Myths: The Israelis, Wagner and the Nazis* (Eastbourne and Chicago: Sussex Academic Press, 2013).

INDEX

Abbate, Carolyn, 30
"absolute music," 16, 39
Adorno, Theodor, 11, 26, 33, 37–39, 65
Aeschylus, 16, 101
Agamben, Giorgio, 127
Anthropocene, 45, 83, 94
anti-Semitism, 1, 7, 9, 13, 130, 131, 134
Appia, Adolphe, 40
Arab Spring, 80
Arendt, Hannah, 47, 132
Asad, Talal, 127
Audi, Pierre, 92

Bagnoli, Enrico, 60–64, 83, 86–87, 101
Barenboim, Daniel, 3, 4, 5–6, 73–74, 92, 117, 134
Baudouin I, King of Belgium, 52
Baudelaire, Charles, 6
Beckett, Samuel, 86
Beethoven, Ludwig, 5, 16, 22, 37, 39, 135
Béjart, Maurice, 57
Bellini, Vicenzo, 15
  Norma, 15, 97, 99, 115–16, 124, 128
Ben-Gurion, David, 134
Benjamin, Walter, 44, 64
Berger, Karol, 74–75, 126
Berghaus, Ruth, 27–28
Berkeley, George, 12
Berlin Conference of 1884, 54, 109
Berlin State Opera (Staatsoper Berlin), ix, 4, 131
Beyreuth Festival, 2, 3, 24, 40, 75, 101
Beyreuth Festival Hall, 37, 46
Bleichröder, Gerson von, 56
Bloch, Ernst, 71
Böcklin, Arnold, 44
Boulez, Pierre, 3, 41
Boym, Svetlana, 20

Brabo, Silvius, 53
Brecht, Bertolt, 59
Broch, Hermann, 11, 32
Burckhardt, Jakob, 31, 47
Burtynsky, Edward, 50, 54, 102

Callas, Maria, 121, 124
Calvin, John, 21
Cassiers, Guy, ix, 3–4, 44–48, 54, 56–57, 60–64, 66, 83, 86–88, 90, 91, 94, 101–102, 109, 113, 114, 115, 118, 120, 122
Cassirer, Ernst, 22
Cather, Willa, 94
Chatwin, Bruce, 32–33, 86
Chekhov, Anton, 10
Chéreau, Patrice, 3, 41–44, 56, 62, 73, 89, 101, 117
Cherkaoui, Sidi Larbi, 57
Conklin, John, 83
Conrad, Joseph, 106–7, 109
Conreid, Heinrich, 133

Dahlhaus, Carl, 14–15, 74
Da Ponte, Laurenzo, 115
Darwin, Charles, 35
Debussy, Claude, 86
D'Haeseleer, Kurt, 101, 122
Dizengoff, Meir, 134
Doniger, Wendy, 91
Donington, Robert, 41
Donizetti, Gaetano, 15
Douglas, Mary, 131, 133
Droysen, Johann Gustav, 16
Durkheim, Emile, 130

Eissler, Kurt, 68
Everding, August, 73

Faisal ibn Abdal-Aziz, King of Saudi Arabia, 52
family romance, 7
Febvre, Lucien, 18
Flimm, Jürgen, 66, 94
Ford, Ford Madox, 107
Forster, E. M.
  A Passage to India, 99–100
Freud, Sigmund, 29, 33, 45, 74, 87, 89, 116, 127, 135

Galeazzi, Francesco, 37
Gennep, Arnold van, 133
Gentlemen's Agreement, 9
Geyer, Ludwig, 55, 69
Ghiberti, Lorenzo, 50
Goethe, Cornelia von, 68
Goethe, Johann Wolfgang von, 23–24, 67–68, 88
Grimm Brothers, 82
Gubanova, Ekaterina, 73
Gulf War (1990), 87–88, 102
Guys, Constantin, 6

Habermas, Jürgen, 84, 88
Haussmann, Baron Georges-Eugène, 53
Hebbel, Friedrich, 44
Hegel, G. W. F., 11, 15, 16, 20–22, 33, 115
Heidegger, Martin, 17, 22, 33, 127
Heinrich, Rudolf, 43
Herz, Joachim, 42–43, 89
Hitler, Adolf, 59, 122
Hochschild, Adam, 53, 108
Hofmannsthal, Hugo von, 71–72, 105
Holzer, Jenny, 63
Homer, 65
Horta, Victor, 51–53
Huberman, Bronislav, 134
Hull, Isabel, 107

Ibsen, Henrik, 43
Israel, and the Wagner taboo, 134–36
Israel Philharmonic Orchestra, 134

Jaws, 89
Jewish Museum Berlin, 1
Jones, Ernest, 29

Kant, Immanuel, 11, 20, 21, 33
Karajan, Herbert von, 110
Kerman, Joseph, 26, 125
Khalid, King of Saudi Arabia, 52
Kissinger, Henry, 56

Kitcher, Philip, 8
Kittsteiner, Heinz-Dieter, 131
Kleist, Heinrich von, 68
Kleist, Ulrike von, 68
Klerkx, Arjen, 101, 122
Konwitschny, Peter, 43
Koselleck, Reinhart, 80
Kovalyov, Vitaly, 73
Kubelik, Rafael, 110
Kupfer, Harry, 43, 73

Lambeaux, Jef, 51–54, 101–2, 104, 106, 108, 109
Lang, Fritz, 44, 90
Lehnhoff, Nikolaus, 129
leitmotif, 24–27, 31–32, 95, 98, 102–3, 132
Leopold II, King of Belgium, 51, 53, 106–7
LePage, Robert, 43–44
Lessing, G. E., 45
Levinas, Emmanuel, 22
Lévi-Strauss, Claude, 27, 41, 133
Lipovšek, Marjana, 73
Lorenz, Alfred, 46
Luther, Martin, 18, 21

Mahavira, 12
Mahler, Gustav, 24
Mahmood, Saba, 127
Mann, Klaus, 109
Mann, Thomas, 9, 70–71, 100
Marx, Karl, 37, 126
Mehta, Zubin, 134
Meier, Waltraud, 118
Meir, Golda, 134
Mendelssohn, Fanny, 68
Mendelssohn, Felix, 7, 8, 68, 69, 129
Mendelssohn, Moses, 56
Metropolitan Opera, 2, 133
Meyerbeer, Giacomo, 7, 8, 69
Michelangelo, 51
Mill, John Stuart, 89
Morabito, Sergio, 43
Mozart, W. A., 26, 68, 105, 115

Napoleon III, 53
Nel, Christoph, 43
Neo-Kantianism, 22
Nietzsche, Friedrich, 2, 3, 11, 12–13, 21, 22, 40, 55, 69, 96, 100, 115–16
Nilsson, Birgit, 110–13
Nitsch, Carl, 67
Nixon, Richard, 56
Nussbaum, Martha, 127

Ovid, 104

Palestine Symphony Orchestra, 134
Pape, René, 73
Peck, Gregory, 9
Peduzzi, Richard, 42
Phillips, Adam, 28–30
postsecular, x, 127

Reformation, 17–18
Resnais, Alain, 59
Roller, Alfred, 40
Rosenberg, Alfred, 24
Rosenzweig, Franz, 33
Ross, Alex, 73–74
Rousseau, Jean-Jacques, 20
Rügamer, Stefan, 57–58
Russell, Anna, 2, 24, 91

Sabean, David Warren, 67–68, 72
Salat, Alfonse, 51
Santner, Eric, 127
Schacht, Richard, 8
Schager, Andreas, 121
Schenk, Otto, 43
Schiller, Friedrich, 40
Schlegel, August and Friedrich von, 68
Schlömer, Joachim, 43
Schmitt, Carl, 127
Schneider-Siemssen, Günther, 43
Schopenhauer, Arthur, 15, 21, 39
Schreber, Daniel Paul, 131
Scruton, Roger, 126
secularization, 19
Shakespeare, William, 16, 85
Shaw, George Bernard, 42, 65, 89, 96–97, 126
Silverman, Debora, 53–54
Sophocles, 65
Stabreim, 16, 59, 84
Stanley, H. M., 107
Storey, Ian, 117–18, 120, 121
Strauss, Richard, 71–72, 105

Tanner, Michael, 126
Taylor, Charles, 127
Tcherniakov, Dmitri, 131

Teatro alla Scala Milano, ix, 4
Third Reich, 4, 134
Thirty Years' War, 18
Thomas, Jess, 112
Toneelhuis Antwerp, 3
Toscanini, Arturo, 134

unconscious, 63, 85, 87, 89–90, 115–17, 125, 135

Verdi, Giuseppe, 73, 117
Visconti, Luchino, 109
Volkov, Shulamit, 8
von Wolzogen, Hans, 24, 132

Wagner, Cosima, 91, 133
Wagner, Richard
  "Beethoven," 15
  Judaism in Music, 7, 9, 130
  Lohengrin, 6, 9–12, 17–18, 63
  Die Meistersinger von Nürnberg, ix, x, 6, 8, 18, 31–32, 40, 79, 99, 134, 136–37
  Parsifal, ix, x, 2, 12, 17, 24, 31, 40, 75, 87–88, 105, 126, 128–32, 133
  Rienzi, 7
  Der Ring des Nibelungen, ix, 2, 3, 6, 7, 8, 24, 30, 33–34
    Götterdämmerung, x, 4, 19, 93, 96–100, 101–25
    Das Rheingold, x, 3, 25, 35–59
    Siegfried, x, 3, 14, 80–81, 82–96
    Die Walküre, x, 2, 3, 5, 14, 27, 55, 60–81
  Tannhäuser, 6, 7, 17
  Tristan und Isolde, ix, x, 2, 6, 10–11, 24, 31, 79, 87–88, 126, 134
Wagner, Wieland, 40, 41, 101
Wagner, Wolfgang, 129
Warburg, Aby, 22, 131
Wauchope, Arthur, 134
Weber, Max, 81, 95, 130, 131, 132
Weizmann, Chaim, 134
Wieler, Jossi, 43
Winnicott, D. W., 9, 29

Zednik, Heinz, 56
Žižek, Slavoj, 59, 127